W.H.Davenport Adams

The Buried Cities of Campania

Or, Pompeii and Herculaneum, their history, their destruction, and their remains

W.H.Davenport Adams

The Buried Cities of Campania
Or, Pompeii and Herculaneum, their history, their destruction, and their remains

ISBN/EAN: 9783337423995

Printed in Europe, USA, Canada, Australia, Japan

Cover: Foto ©ninafisch / pixelio.de

More available books at **www.hansebooks.com**

THE

BURIED CITIES OF CAMPANIA;

OR,

Pompeii and Herculaneum,

THEIR HISTORY, THEIR DESTRUCTION, AND THEIR REMAINS.

By

W. H. DAVENPORT ADAMS,

Author of "*Records of Noble Lives,*" "*Memorable Battles in English History,*"
"*Venice Past and Present,*" &c.

"And in an hour of universal mirth,
What time the trump proclaims the festival,
Buries some capital city, there to sleep
The sleep of ages—till a plough, a spade
Discloses the secret, and the eye of day
Glares coldly on the streets, the skeletons;
Each in his place, each in his gay attire,
And eager to enjoy."
ROGERS.

LONDON:
T. NELSON AND SONS, PATERNOSTER ROW;
EDINBURGH; AND NEW YORK.

1872.

Preface.

SHAKSPEARE makes Malcolm say of the Thane of Cawdor, that "nothing in his life became him like the leaving it." Of Pompeii it may be said, that nothing in its history is equal in interest to its last scene. The fate of the gay Campanian city has been curious. Some cities have secured enduring fame by their commercial opulence, like Tyre; by their art-wonders, like Athens; by their world-wide power, like Rome; or their gigantic ruins, like Thebes. Of others, scarcely less famous for their wealth and empire, the site is almost forgotten; their very names have almost passed away from the memory of men. But this third-rate provincial town—the "Brighton" or "Scarborough" of the Roman patricians, though less splendid and far less populous than the English watering-places—owes its celebrity to its very destruction. Had it not been overwhelmed by the ashes of Vesuvius, the student, the virtuoso, and the antiquary, would never have been drawn to it as to a shrine worthy of a pilgrim's homage. As a graceful writer has justly remarked, the terrible mountain, whilst it destroyed, has also saved Pompeii; and in so doing, has saved for us an ever-vivid illustration of ancient Roman life. Hence the imperishable interest which attaches to it; hence its charm for every cultivated mind. The year-long labours of the most assiduous German commentators could never have thrown such an amount of light upon the manners and customs of the Romans, upon the works of the great Latin writers, as has been accomplished by the spade and pickaxe of the excavators of Pompeii. They show us the theatre, the forum, and the temple—the baker's shop, and the gladiator's training-school—the lady's boudoir, and the wealthy patrician's tablinum,—just as they were when the life and motion of the bright city were suddenly arrested, and its annals abruptly closed. What would we not give for a similar illustration of Egyptian or Assyrian manners! How the historian would rejoice if Persepolis, or Palmyra, or Babylon, could in like manner be restored to the light of day!

It is not the object of the present volume to furnish a hand-book to the ruined city. In the works of Gell, Mazois, Fiorelli, Overbeck, Dr. Dyer, and Nicolini, scarcely a detail has been overlooked; the subject is treated with the most exhaustive minuteness and painstaking research.

The writer's intention in the following pages is simply to furnish a general description of its more remarkable objects, that the reader may form a just conception of their value as illustrative of the customs, arts, and domestic economy of the ancients. Then, if so disposed, he may pursue his studies with the assistance of the writers above mentioned. The excellent work on Pompeii in the " Library of Entertaining Knowledge" is now, to a certain extent, obsolete, and no other compendious summary, in a handy and convenient form, is accessible to the general reader. The writer, therefore, believes that there was a want to be supplied; and he trusts he has succeeded in supplying it, by bringing within a moderate compass the results of the discoveries made at Pompeii and Herculaneum up to the present time. And as his volume is designed for the young, he has introduced concise explanations of various points connected with Roman antiquities, when they seemed needful to a clear comprehension of the subject. Thus: in connection with the baths of Pompeii he has briefly described the general arrangements of the Roman Thermæ, and in connection with its theatres the mode of construction adopted by the ancient architects. The critic will be pleased to remember, however, that these descriptions have been purposely rendered as plain and unadorned as was consistent with accuracy.

Lastly, the writer has to acknowledge his obligations to the authorities already quoted, and especially to Overbeck's "Pompeji." Some admirable photographs of noteworthy buildings and objects, accompanied by agreeable descriptions, will be found in Dr. Dyer's "Ruins of Pompeii;" Sir W. Gell's "Pompeiana" is still a standard work; and the coloured lithographic plates in Nicolini's "Le case ed i Monumenti di Pompeii" are remarkable for their accuracy and spirit.

W. H. D. A.

Contents.

	Page
I. The Destruction of the Cities,	11
II. General View of the City,	47
III. The Forum,	62
The Temple of Venus,	69
The Basilica,	74
The Curiæ, and Ærarium,	77
The Chalcidicum,	77
Temple of Quirinus,	81
The Senaculum,	83
The Pantheon,	84
IV. The Temple of Fortune,	97
V. The Amphitheatres,	103
VI. The Theatres,	127
The Great Theatre,	137
The Small Theatre, or Odeum,	140
The Soldiers' Barracks,	143
Temple of Æsculapius,	145
House of the Sculptor,	145
The Iseon,	146
The Tribunal,	149
VII. The Thermæ, or Baths,	152
Women's Baths,	170
The New Baths,	171

CONTENTS.

- VIII. HOUSES OF POMPEII,
  - The House of the Tragic Poet,
  - House of Ceres,
  - Houses of the Fountains,
  - The Fullonica,
  - The House of Holconius,
  - House of Pansa,
  - House of Sallust,
  - House of the Dioscuri,
  - House of the Centaur,
- IX. THE TOMBS AT POMPEII,
- X. HERCULANEUM,
- XI. RECENT DISCOVERIES,
- XII. THE MUSEUM AT NAPLES.

THE

BURIED CITIES OF CAMPANIA.

I.

𝔈𝔥𝔢 𝔇𝔢𝔰𝔱𝔯𝔲𝔠𝔱𝔦𝔬𝔫 𝔬𝔣 𝔱𝔥𝔢 ℭ𝔦𝔱𝔦𝔢𝔰.

"The long, long night
That followed, when the shower of ashes fell,
When they that sought Pompeii sought in vain:
It was not to be found."
ROGERS.

HE shores of the Bay of Naples exhibit a loveliness and a fertility which have in all ages won the admiration of every lover of the beautiful. On this most favoured region Nature seems to have lavished, with unstinting hand, her choicest gifts. The olive, the mulberry, and the vine adorn its verdant slopes; the bloom of flowers lies on its plains; cool shadows nestle in its leafy woods; its sea shines ever with a tranquil azure; sweet odours are wafted by the breeze from its groves of citron and cedar; and over all the enchanted scene the cloudless heaven extends its arch of serenest blue. Nor are there want-

ing those associations of song and fable which add to the charm of even the fairest landscape. Here Virgil invoked the happy Muses, among fields which seemed consecrated to their worship. On yonder promontory of Misenum lies buried the trumpeter of Hector and Æneas, whose name, as the poet foretold, has become immortal:

> "Æternumque tenet per sæcula nomen."

In the blossomy isle of Æola dwelt the Circean sorceress—

> "The daughter of the Sun, whose charmèd cup
> Whoever tasted lost his upright shape."—MILTON.

At Sorento, which looks out upon the Parthenopean bay from its castled heights, was born Torquato Tasso:

> "Once among
> The children gathering shells along the shore,
> One laughed and played, unconscious of his fate:
> His to drink deep of sorrow, and through life
> To be the scorn of them that knew him not—
> Trampling alike the giver and his gift."—ROGERS.

Gorgeous Roman villas glittered of yore amid the purple vineyards, and the shades of Cæsar and Pompey and Cicero appear ever present to the wanderer's eye. Once again we seem to hear the choral music swelling on the wind, as the gilded galleys of the imperial court glide across the gleaming bay. Yonder convent of Pozzano recalls the memory of its founder, Gonsalvo de Cordova, the great captain. Amalfi, at the mouth of its deep mountain-gorge, revives the history of a maritime republic, which in the eleventh century was the first naval power in Europe. The radiant columns of Pæstum belong to an age which peopled earth with fair

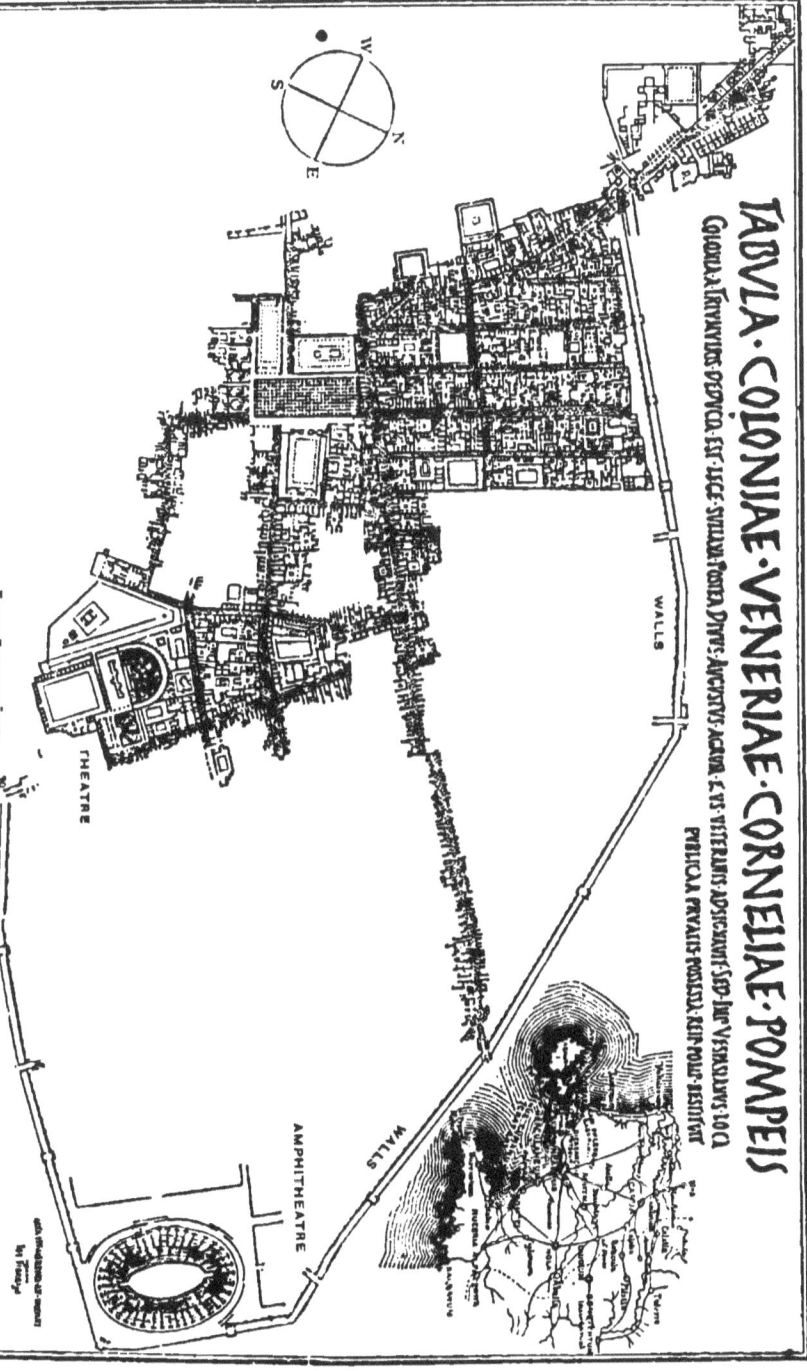

POMPEII BEFORE ITS DESTRUCTION.

creations of god and goddess, nymph and faun. The classic shores are bathed by the Tyrrhene waters; and blue against the eastern horizon lies the syren's isle of Leucosia. At Puteoli stood Cicero's favourite villa, where the Emperor Hadrian is said to have been interred. Westward of Monte Nuovo, and deep hidden among vine-clad hills, sleeps the celebrated Lake of Avernus—

" Where the dark rock o'erhangs the infernal lake,
And mingling streams eternal murmurs wake."—HOMER.

Here, through the cavern of the Sibyl, Æneas descended into the realm of shadows. Cumæ, planted on its volcanic steep, is hallowed by the song of Pindar, who celebrated the great victory of its citizens over the Etruscan armada. At Liternum, cursing an ungrateful country, died the Roman general, Scipio Africanus. And, predominant above all the sweet interchange of cliff, and glen, and plain,—its presence everywhere felt, if not directly seen—a power and a mystery in the landscape which we instinctively recognize,—looms the volcanic mass of mighty Vesuvius, nursing in its heart of hearts the imperishable fire. Viewed from a distance, its flanks covered with wood and grove and bower, crowned with a weird and indescribable beauty—

" An ampler ether, a diviner air,
And fields invested with purpureal gleams"—

it seems as if the stories told of its terrible powers of destruction were all the veriest fables. And yet, smiling as is now the bright Campanian plain, and luminous as are now the soft Parthenopean shores, let but Vesuvius awake in its fury, and all will be changed in a moment to the blackness of desolation.

> "Here verdant vines o'erspread Vesuvius' sides:
> The generous grape here poured her purple tides.
> This Bacchus loved beyond his native scene;
> Here dancing satyrs joyed to trip the green.
> Far more than Sparta this in Venus' grace;
> And great Alcides once renowned the place.
> Now flaming embers spread dire waste around,
> And gods regret that gods can thus confound."—MARTIAL.*

On a slight ascent at the base of this famous mountain stood, upwards of two thousand years ago, a fair and flourishing city, which its inhabitants knew as Pompeii. Its streets sloped towards the right bank of the river Sarno (Sarnus) on the east; on the west and south they inclined towards the very marge of the crater, as, from its cuplike shape, the ancients called the Bay of Naples. Keeping along the sunny strand, the Pompeian might reach, in a couple of hours, the breezy headland, crowned by the temples, theatres, and glittering houses of the sister city of Herculaneum—so named from a tradition that it was founded by the legendary hero Hercules. Both these cities, and the wide stretch of shore between them, were the favourite residence, in ancient days, of the wealthy Romans, who planted their luxurious villas at every vantage-point. You may suppose, therefore, that art bestowed its rarest embellishments on the surrounding landscapes, and that nothing was left undone which could gratify the taste or soothe the fancy. Yet these prosperous and opulent cities no longer seethe with busy

---

* Martial, Epigramm. iv. 44. ("Hic est pampineo virideo modo Vesvius umbris.")

life. Vesuvius still casts its awful shadow over the scene; the air is as sweet and balmy as in times of old; still ripple the "blue Parthenopean waves" on the enchanted strand,—but Pompeii and Herculaneum have ceased to be. From far off lands, which their inhabitants had scarcely heard of, come the antiquary and the scholar, the poet and the artist, to muse amid their ruins. Were they then destroyed by the storm of war, or were their streets swept clean of life by a sudden pestilence? Did their peoples migrate in a body to some wealthier region? Not so. The morning came, and all was bright and joyous. The shops were filled with their usual wares, and crowded by intending purchasers; Campanian peasants stood in the streets with baskets of fruit and flowers; the slaves drew water at the fountains; the gambler rattled his dice; the drunkard quaffed his wine; in the public places gathered the chariots of the wealthy; the priest sacrificed at the altar; the merchant trafficked in the forum; and in the crowded theatre men and women had gathered "with wolfish eyes" to watch the struggles of the athlete and the gladiator in the bloody arena; when, suddenly, a great cloud rose above the crest of Vesuvius in the shape of a pine-tree! The earth shook; the waves rolled to and fro in hasty tumult; darkness swept over the earth; flashes of fire broke through the shrouded sky; showers of stones, and ashes, and fine dust descended heavily and persistently on the plain; rivers of burning, hissing lava, and of steaming mud and water, rolled down the mountain-sides, and poured over the doomed cities in a deluge of destruction! In a few hours the scene was changed, as if some evil spirit had there wrought out its most fatal spells. Commerce and trade, art and science, pleasure and license, honest industry and voluptuous sloth, all were suddenly dissolved! The gambler perished at his dice, the drunkard over his wine-cup. Terrified fugitives, amazed by the darkness, confused by the horror, were cut off in their retreat, and stricken dead. Alas for Pompeii!—it had ceased to be! Alas for Herculaneum!—men knew its place no more! Buried beneath the lava and the accumulated volcanic *débris*, lie temple and circus, the tribunal, the shrine, the frescoed wall, the bright mosaic floor; but there is neither life nor motion in either City of the Dead, though the sea that once bore their argosies still shimmers in the sunshine, and the mountain that accomplished their destruction still breathes forth smoke and fire!

'The story of Pompeii and Herculaneum has been often told; and yet I seek to tell it once again. What I have to say will, however, be said concisely, and in such wise that he who runs may read; while I hope to embody in my narrative the latest results of the research of many trustworthy authorities.

At a very remote period the fertile beauty of the Bay of Naples had induced the adventurous Greeks to settle on its shores. Their seamen had carried home to the states of Hellas the praise of its rich landscapes, its orange groves and violet valleys; nor had they forgotten its manifold capabilities for a maritime and commercial population. It was long before the foundation of Rome that the Greeks, instigated by these reports, planted their colony of Cumæ upon its trachytic hill* and along its sea-girt cliffs.

Ταὶ θ' ὑπὲρ Κύμας ἁλιερκέες ὄχθαι.—PINDAR.

From thence arose many other settlements, either on the Gulf of Puteoli or among the Eubæan hills, on the shores of Gaeta or on the site of the modern Naples. Soon the entire margin of the bay, from Sorrentum to Misenum, was studded by flourishing Greek cities, enjoying a virtual independence, and covering the seas with their armadas. The original Oscan inhabitants of the country were reduced into subjection, and the towns which they had founded were either occupied by the Greeks or acknowledged them as masters. In course of time, it is true, the Oscan language prevailed over that of the invaders, whose inferior numbers were gradually absorbed in the preponderant Oscan population ; but what may be called a leaven of Greek feeling and thought, and Greek perception of the beautiful, existed down to the last hour of the doomed cities.

Pompeii, Oscan in origin, thus became Greek by conquest, and once more Oscan by the force of numbers. It loved, however, to claim for itself a Greek founder, and, without the slightest justification from facts, or even tradition, asserted that it was built by Hercules. The etymology of its name is uncertain, though some authorities consider it to be derived from Πομπεῖα, "storehouses." Its earlier history is as doubtful as its

* Strabo asserts that Cumæ was the most ancient of all the Greek cities in Italy and Sicily.

etymology, and we can only safely assert that it was successively occupied by the Etruscans and the Samnites. The Campanians were conquered by Rome in B.C. 340, but Pompeii preserved its independence for some few years longer. In B.C. 310 it was attacked by the Roman fleet under Publius Cornelius; but the Pompeians repulsed their formidable enemy. Another period of obscurity follows, and we hear no more of the city until the outbreak of the Social or Marsic War in B.C. 91. It had undoubtedly become an ally or tributary of Rome. But it now joined the other Campanian towns in their rebellion, was besieged by Sulla, and only saved from total destruction by the strategy of Cluentius. The Italian general, however, was defeated with great loss at Nola* (B.C. 89). Sulla was prevented from following up his victory by the Marian intrigues in the capital; and to this circumstance may be due the lenient terms which Pompeii secured. At all events, while the other Campanian cities were severely punished, their inhabitants expelled, and Roman colonies settled in their places, Pompeii escaped with the demolition of its fortifications, was admitted to the rank of a "municipium," and suffered to retain its own laws. Sulla, however, placed a military colony (*Colonia Veneria Cornelia*) in the suburbs to overawe the citizens; and frequent collisions ensued between them, necessitating appeals to the Roman senate.

Its delightful situation, its genial climate, and its numerous sources of recreation, soon attracted to it the wealthier Romans. Cicero built himself a villa in its

* Appian, *in Bello Civili*, i. 50

neighbourhood, where he wrote his treatise "De Officiis," and where he held high converse with Hirtius, Balbus, and Pansa. During the Servile War it was the headquarters of Cossinius, one of the legates in the army of the prætor P. Varinius, and Spartacus nearly surprised and captured him while he was bathing in the "Parthenopean waters" (B.C. 73). Augustus planted here a second colony of Roman veterans, in the same suburb as the colony of Sylla, thenceforth named *Pagus Augustus Felix*. Within its walls Claudius found an asylum from the tyrannical vagaries of his uncle Tiberius; and his son Drusus died here in his childhood, choked by a pear which in play he had been throwing up and catching in his mouth (A.D. 20).* The odious oppressions of Sejanus, the infamous favourite of an infamous master, drove to Pompeii for refuge the fabulist Phædrus; and it would appear, from some statements of his own, that in the gay Campanian city Seneca passed much of his studious youth. One of the latest events in its annals was the quarrel between its inhabitants and those of Nuceria (now Nocera), originating in some local sarcasms at a gladiatorial combat which had taken place in the Pompeian amphitheatre. Words led to blows, a battle was fought, and the Nucerians lost the victory. Baffled in the field, they resorted to the council, and laid their complaint before the Emperor Nero, who decided that the Pompeians were in the wrong, and prohibited them from all theatrical entertainments for ten years. Such a sentence remarkably illustrates the importance which the Romans attached to these amuse-

* Suetonius, *Claudius*, 27.

ments, and shows how largely they entered into and made a portion of their daily life. I do not think that the inhabitants of Harrogate or Brighton, for instance, would consider it a severe punishment if their theatres were closed for half-a-dozen decades.

In the Street of Mercury, and near the city wall, there remains to this day, affixed to the side of a house, a caricature or rude drawing scratched on the plaster with a sharp-pointed instrument by some lively Pompeian patriot, in commemoration of this provincial squabble.* An armed figure—apparently a gladiator—is seen descending the steps of the amphitheatre, with a shield in his left hand, and in his right the victor's emblem, a palm-branch. Two rude figures on the left seem intended for a Pompeian conqueror dragging up a ladder his bound and humiliated prisoner. Underneath is written an explanatory legend,—

A POMPEIAN CARICATURE.

"Campani victoria una cum Nucerinis peristis."

Campanians, you perished in victory together with the Nucerians.

This occurred in A.D. 59. Four years later the history of Pompeii was abruptly terminated by an appalling catastrophe—a catastrophe, nevertheless, to which it owes its present fame, and which has communicated to its ruins an importance second only to those of mighty Rome herself. For, while in the Eternal City we find

* Pompeii: "Library of Entertaining Knowledge," i. 36, 37.

our admiration excited by arch, and frieze, and column; by the rent palace and shattered temple—in Pompeii it is our interest that is stimulated by the exhibition of the inner life and daily habits of their builders. It is this, as Dr. Dyer observes, that makes a visit to Pompeii so attractive, that bestows upon it its sole historic value. Rome possesses monuments of surpassing splendour, which leave on the mind of the spectator an indelible impression. Their remains are unequalled; they can never fail to stir the poet's fancy. But they tell us nothing of the home-life of the Romans, of their domestic arrangements and social customs. At Pompeii, on the contrary, their houses are unroofed for our inspection; we may trace their accustomed haunts; we may enter their innermost chambers; we may see the cook at his oven, the wine-vendor in his shop, the noble lady in her boudoir; we may read their electioneering pasquinades, and admire their pictures: it is, in some sort, a realization of the old fable of the Sleeping Beauty,—all vitality, and motion, and energy, after having been suddenly arrested and held in suspense for two thousand years, seem again, at our bidding, to have resumed their wonted course,—

"And all the long-pent stream of life
Dashed downward in a cataract."—TENNYSON.

It has been called a City of the Dead; but the scholar, the artist, the man of vivid imagination and quick conceptions, will easily re-people its silent streets, and re-animate its torpid energies, until, for them, it becomes henceforth a city of the living.

The same great and awful catastrophe which destroyed

Pompeii involved the cities of *Herculaneum* and *Stabiæ* in ruin. The three cities were situated at nearly the same distance from each other: Herculaneum, northwest, on the site now occupied by Portici and Resina, about four miles from Naples; Pompeii, in the centre, on the right bank of the Sarno, six miles from Herculaneum; and Stabiæ, on the lower slope of Monte San Angelo, south, between four and five miles from Pompeii. Herculaneum and Pompeii formed with Vesuvius a triangle, of which the volcano was the apex; the shorter leg between Vesuvius and Herculaneum, the longer between Vesuvius and Pompeii, while the base line might be protracted perpendicularly to Stabiæ. Thus:—

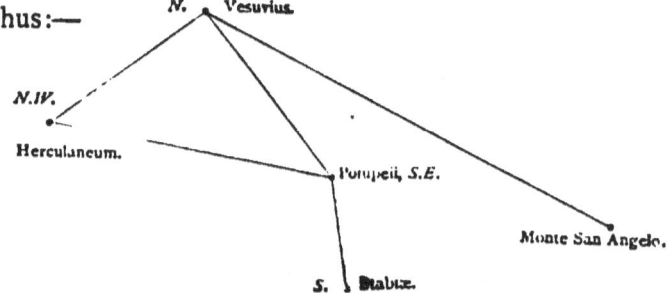

Herculaneum, as already stated, was founded, according to the boastful tradition of its Greek colonists, by Hercules; whence Ovid calls it *Herculea urbs*. It would seem to have been an Oscan settlement, captured by some Greeks from Cumæ, and afterwards occupied in succession by the Oscans, the Tyrrheneans, the Pelasgians, and the Samnites. According to Livy, it was captured from the latter people in B.C. 293 by the Roman consul, Spurius Carvilius, surnamed Maximus. In the Social War it joined the other Campanian cities in their revolt against Rome, but was besieged and captured by Didius, B.C. 80. Like Pompeii, it was admitted to the Roman franchise as a *municipium*, and enjoyed its own local laws and privileges under its Demarchs and Archons. Many splendid villas were erected in its vicinity by the Roman patricians. Servilia, the mother of Brutus, and the favourite mistress of Julius Cæsar, resided here on an estate presented to her by the great Dictator. Its position was particularly healthy, for it crowned a projecting headland between two rivers, and looked across the Bay of Naples in a south-westerly direction. Its port was called *Retina*, a name preserved in the modern *Resina*.

Stabiæ, another of the Greek colonies on this delightful coast, lay on the gently rising ground at the base of Monte San Angelo, commanding a noble panorama of the Parthenopean waters. Little of its history is known to us. It suffered severely in the Social War. Sulla drove out its wretched inhabitants, and supplied their places with a colony of his veterans. The Roman nobles planted their villas all about its environs, in order to avail themselves of its mineral waters, which were praised for their sanitary properties by Pliny and Columella. It was overwhelmed by the eruption of Vesuvius in A.D. 79, when the elder Pliny lost his life, under circumstances to be hereafter related. Its site is marked by the modern port, arsenal, and town of *Castellamare*.

It now seems desirable to furnish the reader with some notes on what may be termed the ancient history of Vesuvius.

The whole region of Campania presents abundant indications of volcanic activity; wherefore the ancients supposed it to have been the scene of the wars between the giants and the gods, and named it *Phlegræi Campi*, the Phlegræan fields (from Hebrew, *Phele Gĕroh*, "marvellous strife"). They invested the entire region with an atmosphere of mysterious fable. The horrors of Tartarus, the ever-burning Phlegethon, the darkness, and the caverns, and the noisome vapours of Hades, were suggested to their lively imagination by its volcanic features. The rent, scorched, and stricken earth, testified to the awful force of Jupiter's thunderbolts. Lake Avernus—"Aornos," the birdless—hidden among the gloom of forests, and subject of old to such mephitic exhalations that no living creature could endure their influence—became the mouth of hell. Under the island of Inarime (Ischia) lay fettered the giant Typhon, or Typhœus, who, vainly rebelling against his chains, shook the earth as with an earthquake.*

> ' And Arime, by Jove's behest,
> Firm fixed on Typhon's monster-breast."—(VIRGIL, *Æneid*, ix. 716.)

And a temple to the omnipotent god of Olympus was reared on the very summit of Vesuvius.

Vesuvius has been for eighteen centuries one of the most active volcanoes in the world. Yet before the Christian era it must have been quiescent for a very long period, as none of the ancient writers record an eruption. They describe it as a volcano, "having cavernous hollows," says Strabo, "in its cindery rocks, which look

* Homer, "Iliad," ii. 782. See also Strabo, book xiii., p. 920.

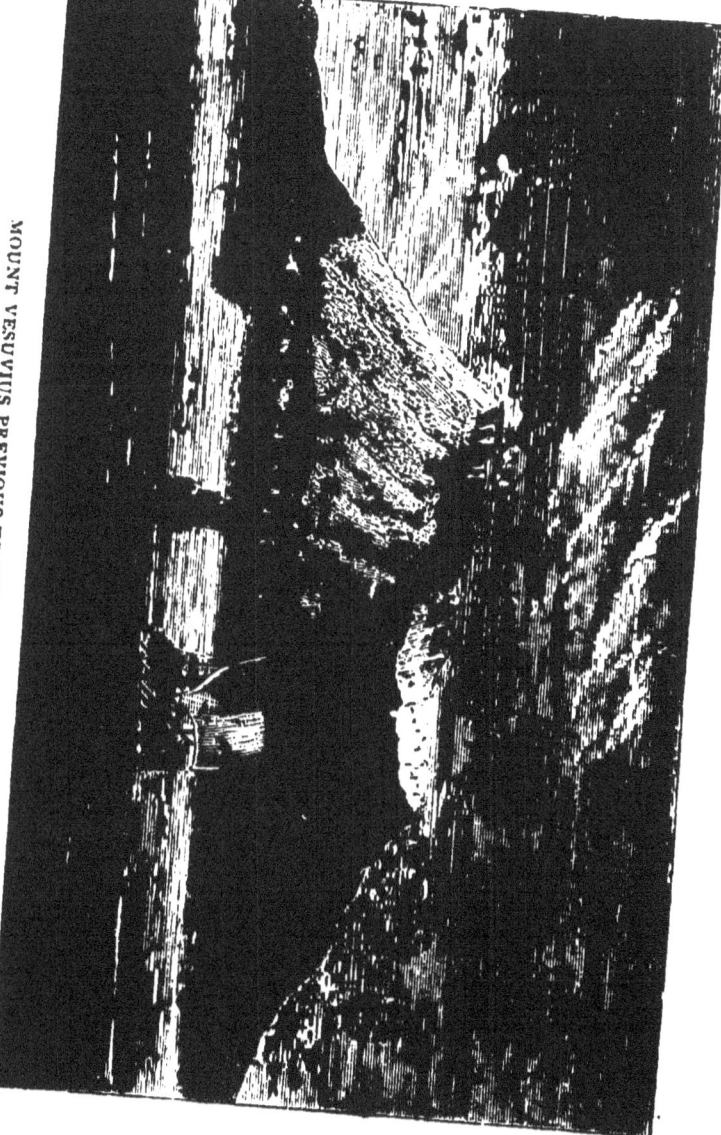

MOUNT VESUVIUS PREVIOUS TO THE ERUPTION OF A.D. 62.

as if they had been acted on by fire." In configuration, the mountain differed greatly from its present outline. Its summit was then level, with a hollow garlanded by wild vines, in which Spartacus and his gladiators posted their camp. The cone, which now forms so conspicuous a feature of it, did not exist, and the circular ridge called Somma, which now encloses it, was undoubtedly a portion of the wall of the ancient crater. Vesuvius was then luxuriantly clothed in vegetation; the vine and the wild olive enriched its rugged flank. Flourishing cities stood at its base. There was no sign of the coming evil.

But in A.D. 63, and in the reign of Nero, the long period of repose was broken, and the latent fires burst forth with terrific violence. An earthquake overthrew a considerable portion of Pompeii and Herculaneum. Scarcely had their inhabitants in some measure recovered from their alarm, and begun to rebuild their shattered edifices, when a still more terrible catastrophe occurred, and the first recorded eruption of Vesuvius, on the 23rd of August, A.D. 79, completed the ruin of the two cities.

Of this event we fortunately possess a singularly graphic description by one who was not only an eye-witness, but well qualified to observe and record its phenomena—I mean Pliny the Younger, whose narrative is contained in two letters addressed to the historian Tacitus.* These letters run as follows:—

"Your request," he writes, "that I would send you an account of my uncle's death [the elder Pliny, author of

---

* C. Plinii Alcib., *Epistolæ*, lib. vi. 16 et 20. The "Epistolæ" have been translated by Lord Orrery, and Melmoth. I follow, to some extent, the version of the latter.

the *Historia Naturalis*], in order to transmit a more exact relation of it to posterity, merits my acknowledgments; for should the calamity be celebrated by your pen, its memory, I feel assured, will be rendered imperishable. .... He was at that time, with the fleet under his command, at Misenum. On the 24th of August, about one in the afternoon, my mother desired him to observe a cloud which seemed of unusual shape and dimensions. He had just returned from taking the benefit of the sun,* and after a cold water bath and a slight repast, had retired to his study. He immediately arose, and proceeded to a rising ground, from whence he might more distinctly mark this very uncommon appearance.

"At that distance it could not be clearly perceived from what mountain the cloud issued, but it was afterwards ascertained to proceed from Mount Vesuvius. I cannot better describe its figure than by comparing it to that of a pine tree,† for it shot up to a great height like a trunk, and extended itself at the top into a kind of branches; occasioned, I imagine, either by a sudden gust of air that impelled it, the force of which decreased as it advanced upwards, or by the expansion of the cloud itself, when pressed back again by its own weight. Sometimes it appeared bright, and sometimes dark and spotted, as it became more or less impregnated with earth and cinders. This extraordinary phenomenon excited my uncle's philosophical curiosity to inquire into it more

---

* The Romans, as one means of preserving their health, were accustomed daily to anoint their bodies with oil, and lie or walk naked in the sun.

† This resemblance has been noticed in later eruptions.

closely. He ordered a light vessel to be got ready for him, and invited me to accompany him if I pleased. I replied that I would rather continue my studies.

"As he was leaving the house, a note was brought to him from Rectina, the wife of Bassus, who was in the utmost alarm at the imminent peril which threatened her; for her villa being situated at the foot of Mount Vesuvius, the only mode of escape was by sea. She earnestly entreated him, therefore, to hasten to her assistance. He accordingly changed his first design, and what he began out of curiosity, now continued out of heroism. Ordering the galleys to put to sea, he went on board, with an intention of assisting not only Rectina, but several others, for the villas are very numerous along that beautiful shore. Hastening to the very place which other people were abandoning in terror, he steered directly towards the point of danger, and with so much composure of mind, that he was able to make and to dictate his observations on the changes and aspects of that dreadful scene.

"He was now so nigh the mountain that the cinders, which grew thicker and hotter the nearer he approached, fell into the vessel, together with pumice-stones and black pieces of burning rock; and now the sudden ebb of the sea, and vast fragments rolling from the mountain, obstructed their nearer approach to the shore. Pausing to consider whether he should turn back again, to which he was advised by his pilot, he exclaimed, ' Fortune befriends the brave : carry me to Pomponianus.'

"Pomponianus was then at Stabiæ,* separated by a

* Now *Castellamare*. (See *antè*. p. 23.)

gulf which the sea, after several windings, forms upon the shore. He had already sent his baggage on board; for though not at that time in actual danger, yet being within prospect of it, he was determined, if it drew nearer, to put to sea as soon as the wind should change. The wind was favourable, however, for carrying my uncle to Pomponianus, whom he found in the greatest consternation. He embraced him tenderly, encouraging and counselling him to keep up his spirits; and still better to dissipate his alarm, he ordered, with an air of unconcern, the baths to be got ready. After having bathed, he sat down to supper with great cheerfulness, or, what was equally courageous, with all the semblance of it.

"Meanwhile, the eruption from Mount Vesuvius broke first in several places with great violence, and the darkness of the night contributed to render it still more visible and dreadful. But my uncle, to soothe the anxieties of his friend, declared it was only the burning of the villages, which the country people had abandoned to the flames. After this, he retired to rest; and it is certain he was so little discomposed as to fall into a deep sleep; for being somewhat corpulent, and breathing hard, those who attended without actually heard him-snore.

"The court which led to his apartment being nearly filled with stones and ashes, it would have been impossible for him, had he continued there longer, to have made his way out; it was thought proper, therefore, to awaken him. He got up, and joined Pomponianus and the rest of his company, who were not unconcerned enough to think of going to bed. They consulted together which course would be the more prudent: to trust to the houses, which now shook from side to side with frequent and violent concussions; or escape to the open country, where the calcined stones and cinders fell in such quantities, as notwithstanding their lightness, to threaten destruction. In this dilemma they decided on the open country, as offering the greater chance of safety; a resolution which, while the rest of the company hastily adopted it through their fears, my uncle embraced only after cool and deliberate consideration. Then they went forth, having pillows tied upon their heads with napkins; and this was their sole defence against the storm of stones that fell around them.

"It was now day everywhere else, but there a deeper darkness prevailed than in the obscurest night, though it was in some degree dissipated by torches and lights of various kinds. They thought proper to go down farther upon the shore, to ascertain whether they might safely put out to sea; but found the waves still extremely high and boisterous. There my uncle, having drunk a draught or two of cold water, flung himself down upon a cloth which was spread for him, when immediately the flames and their precursor, a strong stench of sulphur, dispersed the rest of the company, and compelled him to rise. He raised himself with the assistance of two of the servants, but instantly fell down dead; suffocated, I imagine, by some gross and noxious vapour, for his lungs had always been weak, and he had frequently suffered from difficulty of breathing. As soon as it was light again, which was not till the third day after this melancholy accident, his body was found entire, and free from any sign of violence, exactly in the same posture that he fell, so that he looked more like one asleep than dead."

In his second letter to Tacitus, Pliny relates his own experiences of the phenomenon.

"The letter which, in compliance with your request, I wrote to you concerning my uncle's death, has raised, it seems, your curiosity to know what terrors and dangers attended *me* while I continued at Misenum; for there, I think, the account in my former broke off.

> "'Though memory shrinks with backward start,
> And sends a shudder to my heart,
> I take the word.'*

"My uncle having left us, I pursued the studies which had prevented my accompanying him, until it was time to bathe. After which I went to supper (*ad cœnam*), and from thence to bed, where my sleep was greatly broken and disturbed. For days before there had been some shocks of an earthquake, which the less surprised us as they are extremely frequent in Campania; but on that night they were so particularly violent as not only to shake everything about us, but to threaten total ruin. My mother flew to my chamber, where she found me already rising in order to awaken her. We went out into a small court belonging to the house, which separated it from the sea. As I was at that time but eighteen years of age, I know not whether my behaviour in this juncture may be called courage or rashness; but I took up Livy, and amused myself with turning over that author and making extracts from him, as if all about me

* Virgil, *Æneid*, book ii. (Conington's Translation, p. 35).

had been in full security. While we were thus situated, we were joined by a friend of my uncle's, who had come from Spain on a visit to him; and he, observing me sitting by my mother with a book in my hand, strongly censured her calmness, and reproved me for my careless indifference. Nevertheless, I still went on with my author.

"Day was rapidly breaking, but the light was exceedingly faint and languid; the buildings all around us tottered; and though we stood upon open ground, yet, as the area was narrow and confined, we could not remain without certain and formidable peril, and we therefore resolved to quit the town. The people followed us in a panic of alarm, and, as to a mind distracted with terror every suggestion seems more prudent than its own, pressed in great crowds about us in our way out.

"As soon as we had reached a convenient distance from the houses, we stood still, in the midst of a perilous and most dreadful scene. The chariots which we had ordered to be drawn out oscillated so violently, though upon the most level ground, that we could not keep them steady, even by supporting them with large stones. The sea seemed to roll back upon itself, and to be driven from its strands by the earth's convulsive throes; it is certain, at least, that the shore was considerably enlarged, and that several marine animals were left upon it. On the other side, a black and terrible cloud, bursting with an igneous serpentine vapour, darted out a long train of fire, resembling, but much larger than, the flashes of lightning. Our Spanish friend, whom I have already mentioned, now addressed himself to my mother and me with great earnestness: 'If your brother—and your uncle—is safe,' said he, 'he certainly would wish that you were also; if he has perished, it was his desire, no doubt, that you might survive him; why, then, do you delay your escape one moment?' We could never think of our own safety, we replied, while uncertain of his. Thereupon our friend took leave of us, and withdrew from the danger with the utmost precipitancy.

"Soon afterwards the black cloud seemed to descend and enshroud the whole ocean; as, in truth, it entirely concealed the island of Caprea and the headland of Misenum. My mother implored me to make my escape at any rate, which, as I was young, I might readily do; as for herself, she said, her age and corpulency rendered the attempt useless. But she would gladly meet death, if she could have the satisfaction of seeing that she was not the occasion of mine. I absolutely refused to leave her, and taking her by the hand I led her on; she complied reluctantly, and not without many reproaches to herself for retarding my flight.

"The ashes now began to fall upon us, though in no considerable quantity. Turning my head, I perceived behind us a dense smoke, which came rolling in our track like a torrent. I proposed, while there was yet some light, to diverge from the high road, lest she should be crushed to death in the dark by the crowd that followed us. Scarcely had we stepped aside when darkness overspread us; not the darkness of a cloudy night, or when there is no moon, but that of a chamber which is close shut, with all the lights extinct. And then nothing could you hear but the shrieks of women, the cries of children, and the exclamations of men. Some called aloud for their little ones, others for their parents, others for their husbands—being only able to distinguish persons by their voices; this man lamented his own fate, that man the fate of his family; not a few wished to die out of very fear of death; many lifted their hands to the gods; but most imagined that the last and eternal night was come, which should destroy the world and the gods together.* Among these were some who increased the real terrors by imaginary ones, and made the terrified multitude falsely believe that Misenum was actually in flames. At length a glimmer of light appeared, which we imagined to be rather the foretoken of an approaching burst of flames, as in truth it was, than the return of day. The fire, however, having fallen at a distance from us, we were again immersed in dense darkness, and a heavy shower of ashes fell upon us, which we were at times compelled to shake off—otherwise we should have been crushed and buried in the heap. I might boast that, during all this scene of horror, not a sigh or expression of fear escaped me, had not my composure been founded on that miserable though potent consolation, that all mankind were involved in the same calamity, and that I imagined I was perishing with the world itself!

"After a while, this dreadful darkness gradually disappeared like a cloud of smoke; the actual day returned, and with it the sun, though very faintly, and as when an eclipse is coming on. Every object that presented itself to our

---

* The later philosophers taught that all the world would be destroyed by fire, and that the gods themselves would perish in this final conflagration.

eyes (which were extremely weakened) seemed changed, being covered with a crust of white ashes, like a deep layer of snow. We returned to Misenum, where we refreshed ourselves as well as we could, and passed an anxious night between hope and fear, though, indeed, with a much larger share of the latter; for the earthquake still continued, while several excited individuals ran up and down, augmenting their own and their friends' calamities by terrible predictions. However, my mother and myself, notwithstanding the danger we had escaped, and all which still impended, entertained no thoughts of quitting the place until we should receive some account from my uncle."

The interesting statements of Pliny the Younger have been confirmed in every respect by scientific examination of the buried cities. The eruption of the year 79 was not accompanied by any of those seething rivers of molten fiery lava which have been the principal feature in later outbursts. Pompeii, from its elevated position, could not have been destroyed by lava. It was buried under a mass of calcined pumice-stone—*lapillo*, as the Italians call it—which descended in such amazing quantities as to form an accumulation over the city full twenty feet in depth. Showers of rocks and stones were also among the fatal agents of ruin, and vast streams of water, and of wet sand or mud, which thickened into a species of volcanic paste. This seems to have proved more destructive than the lapillo; for it is evident, from the researches made among the ruins, that many persons who were escaping on the surface of the lapillo, or had sheltered themselves in corners where it could not pene-

MOUNT VESUVIUS AFTER THE ERUPTION.

trate, were overtaken and buried by the mud. The shocks of earthquake killed many—several skeletons have been discovered of persons overwhelmed by a falling wall; while others were suffocated, like the elder Pliny, by the mephitic vapours with which the atmosphere was charged.

The eruption was terrible in all its circumstances—the rolling mud, the cloud of darkness, the flashes of electric fire, the shaking earth—but yet more terrible in its novelty of character and the seemingly wide range of its influence. These combined causes would appear to have exercised a fatal effect on the Pompeians, and but for them nearly all might have escaped. Thus, the amphitheatre was crowded when the catastrophe occurred, but only two or three skeletons have been found in it, which probably were those of gladiators already killed or wounded. The bold, the prompt, and the energetic saved themselves by immediate flight; those who lingered through love or avarice, supine indifference, or palsying fear, perished. A majority of the inhabitants probably took to the sea. Judging from the number of bodies found up to this date, we may infer that out of a population of 20,000, some 2000 fell victims.

Many, to escape from the lapillo, sought refuge in the lower rooms or underground cellars of their houses, but there the steaming mud pursued and overtook them. Had it been otherwise, they must have died of hunger or suffocation, as all avenues of egress were absolutely blocked up. Thus, in the suburban villa known as the "House of Diomed," eighteen persons, mostly women, had gathered in the spacious quadrangular cellar surrounding the garden, but were overwhelmed by the inrush of the destroying flood. "This deluge of fluid matter, which after a time became very tenacious earth, surrounded and enclosed all the substances which it met, and has preserved the impress and mould of them; as, for instance, of a wooden chest, and of a pile of small logs of wood. The same thing happened to the unfortunate human beings who have been discovered; of their flesh nothing has remained but the impress and mould of it in the earth, and within are the bones in regular order. Even the hair on the skulls is partly preserved, and in some cases is seen to have been curled. Of the dresses nothing but the mere ashes have been found; but these ashes preserved traces of the quality of the materials, so that it could be easily seen whether the texture was coarse or fine. Several of the persons had upon their heads cloths which descended to the shoulders; two or three dresses, it would seem, were worn over one another [for the convenience, perhaps, of removing them]; the stockings were of cloth and linen, cut like long drawers; some had no shoes at all. That one woman was superior to the rest could be perceived by the ornaments which she wore, by the fine texture of her dress, and by the coins which were found near her."*

The master of the house, Diomed himself, perished, it is thought, through avarice. At the garden-gate two skeletons were discovered; one, presumed to be Diomed,

---

* Quoted by Dr. Dyer from an Italian periodical, dated December 12th, 1772. For authorities respecting the eruption of Vesuvius, see Landgrebe's elaborate work on Volcanoes.

held in his hand the key; on his finger was a serpent-ring; near him lay about a hundred gold and silver coins. The other, probably a slave, was stretched on the ground beside some silver vases. They would seem to have been suffocated by the vapours while attempting to escape. The incident has been made use of by Lord Lytton in his romance of "The Last Days of Pompeii."

It is difficult, I think, to exaggerate the horrors of *the* last day of the doomed city. The rumbling of the earth beneath—the dense obscurity and murky shadow of the heaven above—the long heavy roll of the convulsed sea —the strident noise of the vapours and gases escaping from the mountain-crater—the shifting electric lights, crimson, emerald green, lurid yellow, azure, blood red, which at intervals relieved the blackness, only to make it ghastlier than before—the hot hissing showers which descended like a rain of fire—the clash and clang of meeting rocks and riven stones—the burning houses and flaming vineyards—the hurrying fugitives, with wan faces and straining eyeballs, calling on those they loved to follow them—the ashes, and cinders, and boiling mud, driving through the darkened streets, and pouring into the public places—above all, that fine, impalpable, but choking dust which entered everywhere, penetrating even to the lowest cellar, and against which human skill could devise no effectual protection;—all these things must have combined into a whole of such unusual and such awful terror that the imagination cannot adequately realize it. The stoutest heart was appalled; the best balanced mind lost its composure. The stern Roman soldier stood rigidly at his post, content to die if discipline required it, but even *his* iron nerves quailed at the death and destruction around him. 'Many lost their reason, and wandered through the city gibbering and shrieking lunatics. And none, we may be sure, who survived the peril ever forgot the sights and scenes they had witnessed on that day of doom!

The Emperor Titus, during his brief but busy reign, contemplated the rebuilding of Pompeii. His scheme, however, was not carried into execution. The inhabitants evicted by the eruption would seem to have made occasional excavations among the ruins to recover what they could of their goods and chattels; and the Emperor Alexander Severus plundered the buried city of many of its finest monuments and columns to embellish his public works at Rome. But the troubles of the empire which afterwards ensued, and the successive irruptions of the Northmen, soon occupied men's minds to such an extent that the fate of Pompeii and Herculaneum ceased to be remembered. Not only their site, but their name, sank into oblivion; although here and there the summit of some of the buildings of Pompeii cropped up above the soil, and the name of *cività*, or the city, which still lingered in the mouths of peasants, might have served to identify its position. After the Renaissance, indeed, references to the buried cities sometimes occur in Italian authors.* Thus: Nicolo Perotto mentions Pompeii, Herculaneum, and Stabiæ in his "Cornucopia," published in 1488; the "Herculaneum Oppidum" is marked in the map of Ambrogio Leone, 1513, as the site occupied by Portici; and Leandro Alberti, in his "Descrizione

* Dr. Dyer, "Ruins of Pompeii," p. 18.

di tulla l'Italia" (1561) recalls the burying of Herculaneum, Stabiæ, and Pompeii by the eruption of Vesuvius, while indicating the spots where they were supposed to have existed. Yet no excavations were made to discover their ruins. Archæology was not then a science. So that when Dominico Fontana, the celebrated Roman architect, carried a subterranean canal from the Sarno to Torre del Greco, actually under the site of Pompeii, and consequently met with the remains of its buildings, inscriptions, and other memorials, no spirit of scientific curiosity induced him to undertake any researches. No lover of antiquity was found to urge the exploration of the vast remains which evidently existed there.*

Herculaneum, though buried under the lava-deposits of several successive eruptions of Vesuvius, was discovered before the sister city, and discovered accidentally.

In 1684 a baker at Portici sank a well on his premises, which, at a depth of ninety feet, terminated near the stage of the Herculaneum theatre. Some twenty-five years later the property was purchased by Prince Emmanuel d'Elbœuf, who prepared to erect a palace upon it. In 1713, while enlarging the well, his workmen found some marbles, with which the prince adorned his walls and staircases. He continued his explorations for five years, and discovered several ancient statues, which, however, were claimed by the Austrian viceroy at Naples, and despatched to Vienna. They were afterwards purchased by Frederick Augustus, Elector of Saxony, and are still preserved in the palace at Dresden.

The excavations were then discontinued until 1736,

* Overbeck, "Pompeji in seinen Gebauden," &c. (2 vols., Leipzig, 1866), p. 35.

when they were renewed by order of King Charles III., and under the direction of Don Rocco Alcobierre, a Spanish officer of engineers, who explored the great theatre, a basilica, and some private houses, but being totally ignorant of antiquities and of classical history, perpetrated the most barbarous mutilations on the valuable antiques which were recovered. While conducting these researches, he was informed by some inhabitants of Torre Annunziata that ancient remains had been discovered about two miles from their town. He accordingly commenced his explorations at the spot now called the Street of Fortune, and was rewarded by finding a skeleton, several coins, and a large fresco painting. Stimulated by this "treasure-trove," he pushed on the works with so much alacrity, that towards the close of 1754 the whole of the amphitheatre was cleared out.

From that time to the present the excavations have been regularly carried on, except for an interval of three years (from 1813 to 1816). The yearly allowance provided by the Neapolitan government was, however, so small, that only a very slow progress could be effected, and not more than one-third of the city has been laid bare in a century! The great theatre was discovered in 1764; the Temple of Isis in 1765 and 1766; in 1766 the Temple of Æsculapius; in 1769 the smaller theatre; the House of Diomed in 1771-1774. The search, for very many years, was conducted in a Vandal spirit, and its sole object was to enrich the royal collection with jewellery, curiosities in gold and silver, statues, and paintings. No pious care was taken of the buildings and monuments of the buried city. No plans were traced of the streets and houses uncovered. The true value of the ruins lay in the life-like pictures they presented of the manners and customs of Roman society, but this was not apparent to the Neapolitan authorities. It is only of late, and under the superintendence of the able and enlightened Cavalier Fiorelli, the present director of the excavations, that they have been conducted in a proper spirit. The frescoes are now very carefully preserved; the buildings, where necessary, restored; plaster casts are taken of the bodies exhumed, and detailed plans made of the streets and public places of the city.

Royal visits to the ruins were formerly very numerous, and on these occasions some object of peculiar interest was invariably discovered. The Emperor Joseph II., on the 7th of April 1769, was accompanied on his progress by his empress, Count Kaunitz, his minister, the king and queen of Naples, Sir William Hamilton, then ambassador at Naples, and several distinguished antiquaries. So brilliant a *cortège* was received by the *genius loci* with becoming respect, and such was the number of articles "found," that the shrewd and energetic emperor could not refrain from hinting to the superintendent, Signor la Vega, that they had been purposely placed there to illustrate the good fortune of sovereigns. La Vega having informed the emperor that only thirty persons were employed on the works, he remonstrated with the King of Naples on the slow progress that must necessarily be made. All would be accomplished by degrees, *a poco a poco*, replied the indifferent Bourbon; whereupon Joseph indignantly exclaimed that three thousand men ought to be employed on so noble an enterprise, which had not its like in any quarter of the globe, and was a special distinction to the kingdom of Naples.

During the reign of Joachim Murat, his accomplished queen, Caroline Bonaparte, frequently visited the ruins. She took a special interest in the progress of the explorations, and it was her patronage that enabled Mazois to commence his superb work on Pompeii. Among other royal visitors may be named Queen Adelaide, the Emperor Francis II., the Grand Duke of Tuscany, the Emperor Alexander I. of Russia, the Grand Dukes of Russia (Alexander II. and Constantine), and King Frederick William of Prussia,—whose names have been bestowed on some of the more notable houses.

Other houses, it should be explained, have been distinguished by the supposed pursuits of their owners, or the interesting articles found within them. Thus, we have the Houses of Diomed, of Sallust, of Pansa, of Cicero, of Rufus, of M. Lucretius, of the Tragic Poet, of the Surgeon, of the Faun, of the Fountain, of the Centaur, of the Painted Columns. In a similar fashion has been determined the nomenclature of the streets.

With these introductory remarks, I proceed to a description of all that is at present interesting in the public and private edifices of the buried city.

II.

General View of the City.

"I stood within the city disinterred,
And heard the autumnal leaves, like light footfalls
Of spirits passing through the streets; and heard
The Mountain's slumberous voice at intervals
Thrill through those roofless halls."

SHELLEY.

OMPEII stood on an insulated hill or plateau of moderate elevation and of an oval shape, surrounded by lava which, at some remote antiquity, had been poured forth from the entrails of Vesuvius. Its highest point was occupied by the Forum. The length of this confined area was about seven furlongs, its breadth under half a mile, its entire circuit nearly two miles. The whole town was surrounded by walls except on the west, where it was sufficiently protected by the steepness of the declivity. It was formerly supposed that the sea washed this side of Pompeii, but on the tract now intervening between the town and the waves Dr. Overbeck has discovered the remains of ancient buildings.* On the east it was bounded by the Sarno, which, now but a shallow rivulet, was formerly navigable for a short distance above its mouth. Three

* Overbeck, "Pompeji," &c.

principal roads approached it: one, from Naples, ran along the sunny coast through Herculaneum, Retina, and Oplontis; a second diverged from the Popilian *Via* at Nola; and the third consisted of two branches from Nocera and Stabiæ, which united into one before reaching the Sarnus.

Thus situated, it seemed to possess all the local advantages which the most zealous citizen could have desired for his birth-place. On the edge of the sea, at the entrance to a fertile plain, on the bank of a navigable river, and at the base of the vine-clad slopes of Vesuvius, it combined the strength and security of a military station with the facilities and conveniences of a commercial town. Its neighbourhood in every direction was studded with glittering villas, and the shore of the "Baian Ocean," even as far as Naples, was so thronged with gardens and hamlets as to appear one city—an Elysian city, bathed in

"The purple noon's transparent light."

It was surrounded—this fair and once-fortunate Pompeii —with *walls* on every side but the western or seaward; these, for the greater part of their circuit, are curvilinear, and without any projecting angles. On the north and north-east they consist of an earthen terrace or *agger*, fourteen feet wide, walled and counter-walled, and ascended from the city by flights of steps, broad enough to admit the passage of several men abreast. The outer face, including the battlement, was about twenty-five feet high, and undefended by a ditch; the inner measured a few feet higher, but was useless in a military sense, though serving to give a more important character to the fortifications. Both walls are built of large blocks of volcanic tufa and travertine, laid in horizontal courses without cement. Here and there patches of later work, known as *opus incertum*, and consisting of fragments of stone and lava embedded in mortar and coated with stucco, have been introduced; to repair, perhaps, the portions injured by Sulla's siege machines.

At intervals the walls were strengthened with square towers, constructed with small rough pieces of tufa, plain in front, but stuccoed and decorated on the sides. Near the western gate they are only eighty paces distant from each other, but towards the east they are planted at two, three, and even four hundred and eighty paces. Each consisted of several stories, had a sally-port, and an archway to enable the troops, when necessary, to move along the agger. About ten are still extant, though sorely dilapidated,—a circumstance which Sir William Gell attributes to injuries sustained in the siege by Sulla at the end of the Social War.

There were eight *Gates*. The most important was that of *Herculaneum*, at the north-west; thrown across the Via Domitiana, a branch of the Appian Way which led to Herculaneum, and thence to Rome. For about a quarter of a mile from the entrance the road is lined with tombs, in accordance with the Roman custom. Hence it is now known as the *Strada delle Tombe*, or Street of Tombs. The gate was double, so as to offer a greater obstacle to assault. The agger was ascended by ten irregular steps, and strengthened by massive buttresses of stone. Like Temple Bar, the Herculaneum gate possessed a large central and two small lateral entrances; the former open to the sky, the latter vaulted; the former measuring 14½ feet broad and 20 feet high; the latter, for foot-passengers, 4½ feet wide and 10 feet high. Passing through the archway, you would see before you a considerable ascent. On the left, outside the gate, stood a pedestal, formerly supporting a colossal statue of bronze, which represented, perhaps, the tutelary deity of the city. There was also a niche where a soldier mounted guard, and the skeleton of one of Rome's legionaries was discovered in it, still grasping his heavy lance, the rusty armour clanking on his fleshless bones. Even the hour of doom, which must have seemed to all the last agony of the suffering earth, had failed to break the rigid bonds of discipline, or shake his blind fidelity to his post. The lightnings shivered, the earth shook, and the hissing rain descended; but enough for him that he had not received permission to escape.

The other gates resembled that of Herculaneum in design as well as in construction. The second led to Vesuvius, whose sides were then clothed with vineyards; the third to luxurious Capua; the fourth to Nola; the fifth was the Gate of the Sarnus; the sixth that of Stabiæ; the seventh, the Gate of the Theatres; and the eighth, the Sea Gate or Porta della Marina, leading to the harbour.

The *Nola Gate* lies within a passage formed of stout masonry, forming a sort of "covered way," which must have proved a dangerous defile to an attacking force. The keystone of the arch is ornamented with a sculptured head and an Oscan inscription; the latter setting forth that the gate was erected by one Vibius Popidius, the Medixtuticus or head-magistrate of the city. Outside the gate was a cemetery, appropriated to the Alexandrian portion of the population.

The *Gate of the Theatres*, excavated in 1851, is of great antiquity. It appears to have been closed with massive double doors. An Oscan inscription in the gateway recorded the names of some of the streets and principal objects in Pompeii.

The entrances to the city now in use are the Herculaneum Gate, the Sea Gate, and the Gate of Stabiæ.

The *Streets* of Pompeii can never have presented a stately or superb appearance, from their extreme narrowness. Excepting the principal thoroughfares, none will admit the passage of two chariots abreast. The widest, including the side footway, does not exceed 93 English feet. Their pavement consists of large irregular pieces of lava joined together with great care ; the ruts worn by Pompeian chariot-wheels are still conspicuous. Their appearance in the old time has been described by Lord Lytton as a scene of " glowing and vivacious excitement," owing, not to any architectural graces, but to " the sparkling fountains, that at every vista threw upwards their graceful spray in the summer air; the crowd of passengers, or rather loiterers, mostly clad in robes of the Tyrian dye; the gay groups collected round each more attractive shop; the slaves passing to and fro with buckets of bronze, cast in the most graceful shapes, and borne upon their heads; the country girls stationed at frequent intervals with baskets of blushing fruit and flowers; the numerous haunts which fulfilled with that idle people the office of cafés and clubs at this day; and the shops, where on shelves of marble were ranged the vases of wine and oil, and before whose thresholds, seats, protected from the sun by a purple awning, invited the weary to rest and the indolent to lounge."*

In the wider streets, stepping-stones are placed at frequent intervals in the centre for the convenience of the pedestrian. On either side runs a kerb, about twelve to eighteen inches high, and separating the foot-pavement from the road. In obedience to a provision of the law of Caius Gracchus, *De viis muniendis*, stones and steps for mounting horses are raised at the edge of the footway, and holes made in the kerb opposite the principal houses and shops for fastening the halters.

Of the streets excavated up to the present date, *five* may be looked upon as the main arteries of the pleasure and business of Pompeii. These are:—

(1.) The *Domitiana*, or *Consularis*, leading from the Herculaneum Gate to the Forum. It receives several minor streets on either hand, forming *Triviæ*, or places where three ways meet;

(2.) The *Street of Abundance*, or of the *Dried Fruits*, only partially revealed to modern eyes, seems to have ran in a straight line from the Gate of the Sarno to the Forum;

(3.) The *Street of the Baths*, of *Fortune*, and of *Nola*, as it is successively called, struck from the Gate of Nola to the sea;

(4.) The fourth led from the Gate of Vesuvius to that of Stabiæ; and

* Lord Lytton, "Last Days of Pompeii," book i., chap. 2.

(5.) The fifth, called in the upper part the *Street of Mercury*, and in the lower, the *Street of the Forum*, passed from the north wall of the city to the Forum,

STRADA DI SALLUSTIO.

and was the busiest, broadest, and most animated of all the Pompeian thoroughfares.

The stranger wandering over Pompeii in search of the curious or interesting, would have had his attention very forcibly drawn to the street literature blazoned on the walls. The Pompeians, for instance, at election time, gave vent to their partizanship, like English electors, in satires and pasquinades. These were painted in large letters in red and black paint, or sometimes scrawled in charcoal. Old advertisements were wiped out with a coat of white, on which the fresh inscriptions were duly recorded. In many cases the new coating has fallen off, revealing the old letters, which are generally in the Oscan character, and belong to a period anterior to the Social War. The activity of Pompeian schoolboys is shown by rude scratchings of Greek letters; the youthful Lepidus endeavouring, it may be, to outvie his comrade Scaurus in illustrating the Greek alphabet.

In the amphitheatre has been found a mass of inscriptions, whose number suggested the following epigram:—

"Admiror paries te non cecidisse r(uinam),
Qui tot scriptorum taedia sustineas."

[I marvel, O wall, that thou hast not fallen into ruin, sustaining as thou dost the tediousness of so many writers.]

The electioneering advertisements are mostly uniform in style, and contain the names of the favourite candidate, and of the persons who support his claims, terminating with the formula O. V. F., that is, *Orant* (or *orat*) *vos faciatis:* in other words—We hope you will appoint so-and-so.* On the wall of the so-called House of Pansa appears the following: "Pansam: æd: Paratus rogat"—Paratus solicits you to appoint Pansa as ædile. From this inscription we might infer that the house where it is found belonged to Paratus and not to Pansa. If

* Overbeck, "Pompeji," ii. chap. 6, pp. 91-115.

Mr. Smith wished to recommend Mr. Brown as vestryman, I do not think he would plaster his bills on Brown's mansion. A curious notice is recorded by Overbeck:

"Sabinum æd[ilem] Procule fac et ille te faciet."
[O Proculus, make Sabine ædile, and he will make thee.]

In our British elections this system of mutual profit is often acted upon, but never, I think, so unblushingly avowed. The epithets bestowed upon the candidates are, of course, eulogistic. The would-be ædile is *bonus, probissimus, verecundissimus, juvenis integer, juvenis egregius, bonus civis, dignus reipublicæ,* and the like.
Here is another example:

"M. Holconium Priscum decemvirum juri dicendo O. V. F. Philippus."
[Philippus beseeches you to create M. Holconius Priscus a decemvir of justice—justice of peace.]

Another inscription runs:

"Marcum . Cerrinium . Vatiam . Ædilem . Orat . Ut . Faveat(is).
Scriba . Issus : Dignus Est."
[The scribe Issus requests you to support M. Cerrinius Vatia as ædile. He is worthy.]

Many of the recommendations proceed from the trade-guilds or corporations, which would seem to have been numerous and powerful at Pompeii. I find mentioned:

Offertores (dyers).
Pistores (bakers).
Cæparii (green-grocers).
Plostrarii (cartwrights).
Piscicapi (fishermen).
Forenses (lawyers).
Saccarii (sugar-dealers).
Fullones (fullers).
Perfusor (perfumer).

Aurifices (goldsmiths).
Pomarii (fruiterers).
Lignarii (wood-vendors).
Salinenses (salters).
Agricolæ (husbandmen).
Muliones (muleteers).
Culinarii (cooks).
Lanifricarius (a wool-washer).
Caupones (innkeepers,.

These titles have suggested to the street wits of Pompeii an occasional squib, and recommendations are set forth from the *scribibi* (late tipplers), the *dormientes universi* (all the free guild of slumberers), and the *pilicrepi* (or ball players). Some pedantic schoolmaster is made to come forward with wretched grammar: *Valentius, cum discentes suos* (Valentius and his pupils).

The *graffiti* (inscriptions scratched with a sharp instrument on the stucco), and the more ambitious painted legends, are of the most various character, embodying a puff, a notice, a wise saying, a jest, a quotation from popular poets, or an amateur essay in versification. Occasionally they indulge in satirical depreciation of— let us say—Aliquis for not inviting Nemo to supper; or they praise Rufus as a liberal host; or they express his love for the beautiful Lalage; or bring the public acquainted with the state of his health. Often the first inscription receives its comment in another, just as in Hotel Albums or Visitors' Books one traveller records his opinion of the remark of his predecessor. Within the houses they have usually a domestic character. The mistress jots down the birth-day of her eldest son, or the number of tunics and togas sent to the dyer or the washerwoman, or the daily consumption of oil and wine.

GRAFFITE, OR WALL CARICATURE IN POMPEII.

The Winchester school-boy will be reminded of the

famous "Aut disce, aut discede; aut memet suo tertia cædi" (Learn or go; the third alternative is to be flogged), by the following :—

"Otiosis hic locus non est, discede morator."
[This is no place for the idle—let the dawdler begone!]

And just as Mr. Webster or Mr. Buckstone advertises the performance at the Adelphi or the Haymarket, a keeper of gladiators in the *Strada degli Augustali* announces,—*

" A. Suettii Certi ædilis familia gladiatoria pugnabit Pompeis pridie Kalendas Junias; venatio et vela erunt."
[The gladiator company of the ædile Certus will fight at Pompeii the day before the Kalends of June; there will be a venatio and awnings.]

To another announcement is added " qua dies patentur," equivalent to our English " weather permitting."
I transcribe from Overbeck a few of a poetical cast :—

"Quid pote tam durum saxso aut quid mollius unda?
Dura tamen molli saxsa cavantur aqua."
[What so hard as stone, what softer than water! Yet the hard rocks are hollowed by the soft water.]

This Ovidian couplet has been wrongly spelt by some poetical Pompeian. A more original mind has trusted to his own resources, and favoured posterity with,—

"Alliget hic auras si quis obiurgat amantes
Et vetet assiduas currere fontis aquas."
[If any one can restrain the lover, he may also bind the breezes, and forbid the perennial spring to flow.]

A hungry diner-out exclaims,—

" L. Istacidi! At quem non cænæ barbarus ille mihi est!"
[L. Istacidius! What a barbarian not to ask me to supper!]

* Overbeck, " Pompeji," ii. 99 (Leipzig, 1866).

Love seems to have entered largely into Pompeian life, for a majority of the inscriptions refer to the universal passion. How the boys of London would titter if they saw written on a " dead wall " some such effusion as the following :—

" Methe Cominiaes atellana amat Chrestum corde, sit utreisque
Venus Pompeiana propitia et semper concordes veivant."
[Methe, the slave of Cominia, loves Chrestus with all her heart: may the Pompeian Venus be propitious to both, and may they always live happily together !]

On the wall of the peristyle of the corner-house in the Strada della Fortuna and Vicolo dei Scienziati is scratched a record of the spinning-tasks allotted to the female slaves, with the weight of wool for each (*spensa*, spelt *pesa*). Their names were,—Vitalis, Florentina, Amaryllis, Januaria, Heracla, Mária (female of Marius), Lalagia (compare Horace's Lalage), Cerusa, Damalis, and Doris.*

Having satisfied himself with these specimens of the street literature of Pompeii, our wanderer may next direct his observations to the shops. To see the best of these he will have to enter the Strada dell' Abondanza, also called the Street of the Silversmiths; but they are nowhere equal to the shops of a second-rate street in an English provincial town. They were usually built round the houses of the wealthier classes, whom they furnished with a very respectable income. From an inscription at Pompeii we learn that one Julia Felix was the owner of nine hundred. The walls were painted in gaudy colours; the tradesman's sign was placed over his door; the whole front was open, but closed at night by shutters, which

* Overbeck, " Pompeji," ii. 112, 113.

A BAKER'S.

slided in grooves cut in the lintel and basement wall before the counter, and by the door.

Here is the shop of a *pistor*, or baker. Let us enter. The oven is placed at the end of the counter furthest from the street. The three steps on the left are crowded, you see, with different sorts of measures.

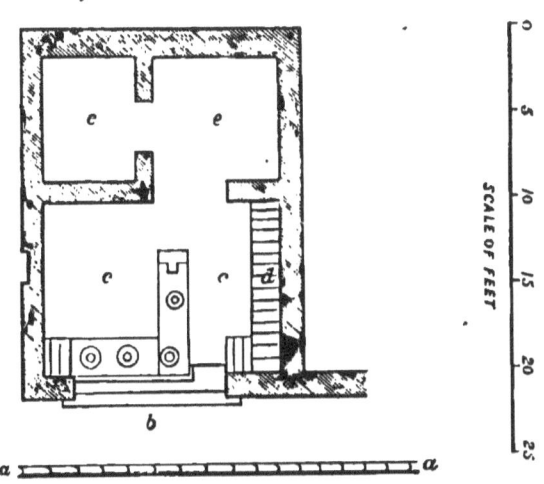

a. The kerb, with holes for fastening the halters of horses and mules.
b. The foot-pavement.
c. The shop.
d. Staircase, leading to upper story.
e. Back rooms (very small).

It may here be noted that the Pompeian bakers or cooks were celebrated for their manufacture of a pickle called *garum*, which was made of the entrails of fish macerated in brine. It was sold at the rate of a thousand sesterces for two congii, or about £4 a gallon. An inferior kind, called *alec*, was made with anchovies.* The shop we are now examining appears to have been a depôt for the sale of this and other liquids, of dressed and

* Pliny, "Natural History," xxxi. 43.

undressed provisions. The rooms at the back of the shop are of insignificant dimensions. A staircase in the corner leads to an upper story.

A corner shop near the Forum seems to have been a *Thermopolium*, or shop for the sale of hot drinks. Its walls are brightly painted in blue panels with vermilion borders; slabs of marble line the counter. A curious

THERMOPOLIUM AT POMPEII.

machine for the preparation of warm drinks has been discovered. It may be compared to a modern urn or tripod, supported by three legs. A section of it, with its conical cover, is shown in the accompanying illustration: $a\,a$, is the body of the urn: b, a small cylindrical furnace in the centre; it has four holes in the bottom, as shown in the plan at g, to provide for the escape of the ashes.

A CURIOUS UTENSIL.

and to create a draught: *c*, is a vase-shaped mouth, through which the water was poured in, serving also for the emission of steam: *d*, a tube which, by means of a cock, served to let off the warm liquid; it is placed thus high to prevent the pipe being stopped up by the ingredients decocted: *e*, is a conical cover, whose hollow is closed by a thin and somewhat concave plate: *f*, a movable flat cover, with a hole in the centre, which closes the whole urn except the mouth of the small furnace: *n n*, nuts and screws to fasten this movable cover on the rim of the urn: *i i*, the rim, convex externally, and concave internally, which, the cover being put on, receives into its concavity the rim of the mouth of the furnace.*

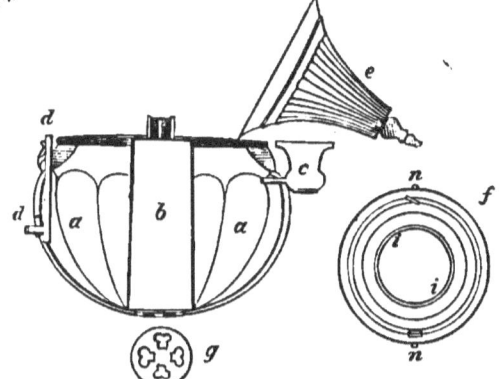

The shops in Pompeii are all of the same character, differing only in size, fittings, and decorations. We may therefore betake ourselves in the next place on a visit to the public buildings of the city; among which the Forum will necessarily claim our earliest attention.

* Pompeii (in "Library of Entertaining Knowledge"), vol. i. p. 127. See also Donaldson's "Pompeii."

III.

The Forum.

> "In many a heap the ground
> Heaves, as if Ruin in a frantic mood
> Had done his utmost. Here and there appears,
> As left to show his handiwork, not ours,
> An idle column, a half-buried arch."
>
> ROGERS.

N the old days of Roman power, the Forum, in every Roman city, was the great centre of business, of pleasure, of the public life of the people. It served alike for commercial purposes and for the administration of justice; it was a market, an Exchange, a place of civic assemblage. It included our Law Courts, our Public Halls, our Westminster Abbey, our Houses of Parliament, our Newgate and Covent Garden Markets, in one common enclosure. There the idler gossipped with others as indolent as himself; there the merchants trafficked; there the orator harangued; there the decemviri decided the cases brought before them; there you might buy the piscatory products of the Mediterranean, or rare fruits and dainties from Candia or Cyprus. Under the porticoes were gathered various trades: the money-changers clinked their glittering coins in the stalls below; in the tabularia were ex-

FORUM OF POMPEII.

hibited the public records; the prætor sat in the basilica to administer the laws. It is impossible to imagine a scene more animated or interesting than the Forum at Pompeii must have presented in the brightest period of its history. Under a cloudless sky of blue was transacted all the business of life, and at this elevated central-point concentrated those who lived to toil, no less than those who lived to make a toil of pleasure. The semi-maritime, semi-luxurious character of Pompeii, which was both a commercial port and a fashionable watering-place, lent a peculiar aspect of gaiety to the spectacle; for in the same crowd mingled the Roman patrician, the graceful Greek, the Alexandrian, the Cypriote, the Jew moneychanger, their various costumes radiant with many colours.

Most of the streets of Pompeii led up a considerable ascent to the elevated site of the Forum, which was distant about four hundred yards from the Herculaneum Gate and from the Great Theatre.

It is surrounded on three sides by Doric columns of grayish-white limestone, each column being about 12 feet in height, and 2 feet $3\frac{1}{2}$ inches in diameter. Above this colonnade was formerly a gallery. On the east stood a more ancient arcade, with Doric columns of tufa, which, having been injured by the earthquake of 63, was rebuilding at the time of the last great catastrophe. The open central area was paved with slabs of limestone. In front of the columns, and of the southern and western porticoes, stood ornamental pedestals of white marble, which, when crowned with statues—some of them equestrian—must have contributed materially to the beauty and interest of the spot. They are decorated with a

Doric frieze, and one still retains its dedicatory inscription:—*

<pre>
       C. CVSPIO. C. F. PANSÆ
       II. VIR. J. D. IVART. QVING.
       EX. D. D.   PEE. PVB.
</pre>

The names of eminent Pompeian citizens are inscribed upon other pedestals, including Sallust, Gellianus, Rufus, Scaurus.

At the north end of the Forum stands the TEMPLE OF JUPITER, raised upon an elevated basement, and occupying a position which renders it dominant over the whole city, like the Temple of the Capitoline Jove at Rome. It is prostyle (προ, and στύλος), that is, it has a detached columnar portico in front; of the Corinthian order; the columns are pycnostyle (πυκνὸς, and στύλος), or placed close together; while the portico is hexastyle, or embellished with six columns in front, and three at each side. These columns are of the fluted Corinthian pattern. A row of pillars runs on each side along the interior of the cella (or nave), which seems to have been open to the airs of heaven. It is probable that there were two ranges of columns within the cella, one above another, and that the floor of a gallery rested on the lower tier. The clear space or open area of the said cella was about 42 feet by 28 feet 6 inches. The interior has been painted, chiefly in black and red. A broad border of black and white mosaic encloses the pavement, which is formed of lozenge-shaped pieces of marble. The entrance is approached by a flight of steps, ornamented with pedestals for colossal statues. Exclusive of this approach, it mea-

---

* Sir W. Gell, "Pompeiana," i. 32.

sured 100 feet in length, and 43 feet in width. Its total height, including the basement, was about 60 feet.

When exhumed in 1817–18 many relics of the past were discovered among its ruins. There was a colossal head of the god whose worship was conducted within the fane; a votive offering, in bronze, of a woman carrying her infant; a torso of good workmanship, with a statue outlined on its back, and intended to have been cut out of it; a bronze helmet; a patera; a plate; and two skeletons, one of which had been crushed in the middle by the falling of a marble column;—mute yet eloquent witnesses of the sudden destruction which fell upon the unfortunate city!

A low brick arch, adjoining the south-western end of the basement, opens into the Prisons—dark, narrow, windowless dungeons, whose only light was the faint glimmering that penetrated through the iron grates of the doors. Several skeletons were found in them, with rusty shackles still encircling their leg bones. When the fire and the cloud fell upon Pompeii, the gaolers escaped, giving never a thought of the terrible fate to which they abandoned the inmates of their gloomy cells.

At the other angle of the temple stands a gateway, which was evidently intended as a triumphal arch. Its massive piers, and part of the columns that embellished them, remain. In each pier were two attached fluted Corinthian columns of white marble, excellently wrought. Between them was a square-headed niche, inclosing statues; one of which seems to have been connected with a fountain, the water flowing from a vase or cornucopia placed in the hands of the figures.

The ancient Romans loved the music and the sparkle of running water, and adorned their cities plenteously with "silvery shafts of spray," which gave a delightful coolness to the air and a grateful pleasure to the senses. Statues, chiefly of bronze, applied to this purpose, were numerous at Pompeii. Among others have been found two boys, of exquisite workmanship, carrying vases on their shoulders, and two others holding masks, both masks and vases resting on pedestals. Water was carried through the figures in leaden pipes, and allowed to run in a glittering stream through the masks and vases.

Adjoining the prisons stood a long narrow edifice used as a *granary* or *store-house;* and in a recess under the colonnade of the Forum were found the public measures for grain, oil, and wine. The measure for grain consists of a thick horizontal slab of stone, pierced perpendicularly by two inverted cones, truncated at the smaller end. Underneath were placed the baskets or sacks, and a flat piece of wood was held in such wise as to prevent the grain from escaping at the bottom, until, the measure being full, the contents, on the removal of the wood, fell into the proper receptacle. "Bonucci mentions a stone," says Sir William Gell, "in the Royal Museum at Naples, which contains measures of liquids as well as of solids, and with the names of the magistrates to authenticate them. Such public measures were probably common to all the cities of antiquity. Travellers may observe one of these stones in a wall near the north gate of Fondi; and another, with three different measures, on the ground near that of Naples." *

* Sir W. Gell. "Pompeiana," i. 33.

TEMPLE OF VENUS.

The reader must understand that the buildings I have now described are all situated on the north side of the Forum. Let him suppose that we next continue our journey of exploration along its western border, facing towards the city and the distant Mediterranean. After passing the granary he will see, on the right, the largest and most magnificent of all the Pompeian buildings,—

THE TEMPLE OF VENUS.

Antiquarians are not agreed, it is true, upon its proper appellation. When first discovered it was considered to be a temple of Bacchus, from two pictures of a Bacchic character which were found within its inclosure. It has also been called the House of the Dwarfs, from a series of quaintly humorous dwarf figures painted on the wall. But when we consider that Venus was the patron goddess of Pompeii, we may reasonably infer that to her worship and in her honour would be dedicated the superbest temple. Moreover, a statue of the ideal beauty, recalling in its modest expression * the famous *chef-d'œuvre* at Florence,—

> "There, too, the Goddess lives in stone, and fills
> The air around with beauty; we inhale
> The ambrosial aspect, which, beheld, instils
> Part of its immortality"—

that Medicean statue which has "charmed the world" —and a bust of the goddess, found in the cella,—would seem to confirm this supposition.† And if the following

---

* M. Marc Monnier, "Pompéi et les Pompéiens" (in "Tour du Monde"). vol. v., p. 393.
† Overbeck, "Pompeji," i. 101.

translation of an inscription discovered on the spot be correct, the question need not further be discussed :

    M. HOLCONIVS . RVFVS . D. V. I. D. TER.
    C. EGNATIVS . POSTHVMVS . D. V. I. T. TER.
    EX . D. D. IVS . LVMINVM.
    OPSTRVENDORVM . HS. ∞ ∞ ∞
    REDEMERVNT . COL. VEN. COR.
      VSQVE . AD . TEGVLAS.
      FACIVNT . CURARVNT.

[Marcus Holconius Rufus and Caius Ignatius Posthumus, decemvirs of justice for the third time, by a decree of the Decurions, bought again the right of closing the openings for three thousand sesterces, and took care to erect a private wall to the collegium of the incorporated Venerei up to the roof.]

It has been remarked that these openings were probably between the massive piers on the side next the colonnade of the Forum, and that, previous to their being closed, the public could see into the area surrounding the fane of Venus. As the rites of the goddess were too frequently of a licentious character, one can easily understand why the magistrates would wish to shut them off from the public gaze.

Let us now endeavour to restore the Temple in all its pristine magnificence.

An open area, 150 feet long by 75 feet wide, is surrounded by a peristyle of forty-eight marble columns, forming a portico or arcade between thirteen and fourteen feet in breadth. The columns are painted yellow in the lower portion, and white in the upper. They were originally Doric, but, as you see, have been altered to Corinthian, the prevailing fashion, and clumsily spoiled in the alteration. In one of them a perforation has been made to receive the pipe which conducted water for the sacrifices into a basin placed upon a circular fluted pedestal. A consular figure was found here, and it has been supposed that a similar figure was placed before each column of the colonnade.

At the upper end of this open area stands the Temple, upon an elevated basement. You ascend to it by a flight of eleven steps, in front of which is placed a large altar, covered with a slab of black lava. According to some authorities, its form is only adapted for offerings of cakes, fruit, and incense, the usual offerings to Venus; but others assert that the slab, when exhumed, contained three receptacles for fire, and that the ashes of victims were discovered on it. An inscription on the east side, repeated on the west, records that the quartumviri, M. Porcius, M. F. L. Sixtitius, L. F. Cn. Cornelius, and Cn. F. A. Cornelius, erected it at their own expense.

The walls under the colonnade are vividly painted in many colours, representing, on a black ground, villas and landscapes, dwarfs, pigmies, battles with crocodiles, dancers, sacrifices to Priapus, and various designs of an Egyptian character; which would seem to show that eventually the worship of Osirei had been combined with that of Venus. Within the cella, which is small, was found a beautiful mosaic border, and, in an apartment beyond, an admirable fresco of Silenus playing on the lyre to the Infant Bacchus. This had been removed from some other place, and carefully fastened in its present situation with iron cramps and cement.

Continuing our circuit of the Forum, we next arrive,

on the western side, at the Basilica; but may pause for a moment to survey once again the animated spectacle which the crowded area presents.

In yonder stalls, with their glittering heaps before them, sit the money-changers, trafficking with busy mer-

FRESCO. A LANDSCAPE (FOUND AT POMPEII).

chants, and with seamen, noticeable for their diversities of costume—Greeks from the Ægean, Asiatics from the shores of Asia Minor, Tunisians, and Egyptians from the mouth of the Nile. The lawyers and the clients, clothed in long togas, are streaming in a ceaseless procession towards the seats of the magistrates; for Law had its priests, its worshippers, and its victims in the first as well as in the nineteenth century. Under the Doric colonnade stand several idlers, refreshing themselves with a light repast of pieces of bread soaked in diluted wine, and discussing with eager gossip the last bit of scandal or the latest news arrived from Rome. In the open space various petty traders are exercising the arts of their calling. One man recommends his ribbons to a country dame; another sells to a Campanian peasant a pair of heavy shoes; a third supplies hot drinks from his small and portable stove; a fourth is a schoolmaster, expounding to his puzzled scholars the mysteries of the Greek alphabet. In the gallery above have collected the more opulent citizens of Pompeii, intent, as their grave countenances show, upon serious business.

Lo now! the crowd gives way, and through the respectful throng some senator advances to join his illustrious *confrères* in the Temple of Jupiter. In and out of the public granaries pass the corn-dealer and the wine-seller, to measure their respective wares, and negotiate their sale or exchange. Merrily murmurs the fountain in the niche of yonder arch, on whose bronzed and equestrian statue of Caligula the sunshine glances and shimmers. The poorer citizens, with panniers under their arms, force their way through yonder small vestibule into the Pantheon, where the priests, at a platform placed between two columns, have exposed for sale such provisions as they could rescue from the sacrifice.

Nothing, in a word, can exceed in variety—as Lord Lytton remarks*—the costumes, the ranks, the manners,

* Lord Lytton, " Last Days of Pompeii," bk. iii. c. 1.

the occupations of the crowd; nothing can exceed the bustle, the gaiety, the animation, the flow and flush of life all around. You see here all the myriad signs of a heated and feverish civilization, where pleasure and commerce, idleness and labour, avarice and ambition, mingle in one gulf their motley, rushing, yet harmonious streams.

So we follow the togaed train of lawyers into

THE BASILICA.

The idea of a Basilica was of Greek origin. This, indeed, might be inferred from its name: Βασιλική (sc. στοά), a regal portico, where the Athenian "King Archon" (Archon-Basileus) sat to administer justice publicly. The first erected at Rome was built by Marcus Porcius Cato, the censor, about 182 B.C.; and was quickly followed by the Basilica Fulvia, the Basilica Sempronia, and, under the Empire, the Basilica Julia, the Basilica Ulpia of Trajan, and the Basilica of Constantine. It was invariably of an oblong form, its breadth not more than one-half, and not less than one-third of its length. A gallery ran around it; an apsis, or recess, either square or circular, terminated its further extremity; and it was usually open to the sky, or only partially roofed. In the apse was placed the judge's tribunal, separated by a railing from the other portions of the building, which were devoted to the same purposes as our modern Exchange. Sometimes, as in the Pompeian Basilica, there was no apse, and the magistrate's court was then cut off from the nave. The upper gallery was thrown open to the public; one-half to the men, one-half to the women. As our Christian churches have been imitated from these Basilicas, the reader who would gain a clear conception of their arrangement has only to suppose a church unroofed, leaving the nave open, but the aisles covered, and in the place of the altar or communion-table, to substitute the judge's curule chair, and the seats of the *judices*, or jurymen.

The Pompeian Basilica—the most perfect example of the kind in existence—measures 220 feet in length by 80 feet in breadth. It is entered through a vestibule having five doorways of masonry, in which grooves have been cut for the insertion of wooden door-jambs. From the vestibule a flight of four steps leads into the interior by five entrances. The open central area is enclosed by a covered gallery resting on a range of twenty-eight fluted Ionic columns, of large size, and constructed of brick and tufa, covered with stucco, forming below a colonnade or aisle, where the merchants and lawyers might shelter themselves from the weather.

The prætor's tribunal, situated at the further extremity of the peristyle—for in the Basilica at Pompeii there was no apse—is a platform, six or seven feet high, ascended by wooden steps; it is decorated with small columns, between which, at the back, small apertures may be seen, and at the sides closets, probably for the magisterial robes.* Temporary cells for the accused were placed underneath; and through two orifices in the floor orders were transmitted to those who had them in charge. A bronze statue stood on a pedestal in front of the

* "Pompeii" (Library of Entertaining Knowledge), i. 137.

tribunal; on each side of which were two enclosed apartments, designed, we may suppose, for the accommodation of the suitors and their advocates, the lictors, officers, and attendants of the court. The interior walls were painted in various colours to imitate marble. That loiterers might be found in the Pompeian public places, as in those of London and Paris, is attested by the numerous inscriptions rudely scratched upon these walls; inscriptions which show that a very low state of moral feeling prevailed among the citizens. One, however, of simple character, is valuable in connection with the supposed age of the Basilica. It runs,—

C . PVMIDIVS DIPILVS HEIC FVIT A D V NONAS OCTOBREIS
M . LEPID Q CATVL COS.

It matters little to the world at large that Pumidius Dipilus was in the Pompeian Basilica on the 3rd of October, but the circumstance of his recording the date —in the year that Lepidus and Catulus held the consulship, or 79 B.C.—proves that the building was erected eighty or ninety years, at all events, before the Christian era.* The name of this idler has thus been preserved nearly two thousand years.

At the south-west corner of the Forum, beyond the Basilica, are two houses which, having been excavated during the rule of the French general Championnet at Naples, are known as the Houses of Championnet. I shall refer to them in a later section of this volume.

Proceeding along the *southern* side, opposite the Temple of Jupiter, we come to three halls of nearly

* Overbeck, "Pompeji," i. 134.

equal dimensions, which, in the absence of all inscriptions to afford a clue to their destination, have been termed

THE CURIÆ, AND ÆRARIUM.

The central one, which has a square recess, and the remains of a raised basement at the end, is called the Ærarium, or Treasury, because some two or three hundred coins were found in it. The side buildings, which have *apsides*, or circular recesses, are supposed to have been the *Curiæ*, or courts where cases of minor importance were decided by the municipal magistrates. They appear to have been richly embellished with marbles, frescoes, and statues.

Proceeding along the eastern side of the Forum, we pass a corner building, whose uses are wholly unknown. It is generally called, but on no good foundation, the Public School of Verna, from an inscription of a certain Verna soliciting the protection of Cœlius Capella, the Decemvir of Justice.

Next to it stands

THE CHALCIDICUM,

or Crypto-Porticus of Eumachia, a large and imposing structure, in the form of a basilica, 130 feet long, and 65 feet broad, which is supposed to have been the Cloth Exchange of Pompeii.* It has two entrances, one from

---

The youthful reader, amazed at the uncouth words, will inquire their meaning. A *crypto-portico* (from κρυπτος, hidden) is a gallery, in which the columns in the interior are replaced by walls, merely pierced for windows. A *chalcidicum* (from the Eubœan city, Chalcis) is an apartment separated by a partition from the body of a basilica, or other large building. It may also be taken to signify any large portico, but antiquaries still differ upon the exact meaning of the term.

the Forum, and the other from the Strada dell' Abondanza. The former was graced with a handsome portico of eighteen columns, which was surrounded by raised platforms, for the convenience probably of haranguing an audience sheltered from the weather, or for the proclamation of edicts and decrees relative to commercial matters.*

The entrance to the central area is through a passage, on each side of which are other passages, with a staircase on the right leading to upper galleries. The Chalcidicum is approached from the Strada dell' Argentarii (Street of the Silversmiths), forming the southern boundary of the building. Here is a small chamber for the custos, or porter, through which may be seen a flight of steps ascending to the floor of the Chalcidicum and Cryptoportico; the wall on either side is painted in black panels, divided by red pilasters. Under the staircase are the remains of a *thermopolium*, whose characteristics I have already described.

The building, as a whole, consisted of a *hypæthrum*, or open court; a portico of forty-eight marble columns; a chalcidicum, or enclosed apartment, at the further extremity; a semicircular recess at the end, containing a statue of Concord; and a crypto-porticus. The latter ran round three sides of the building—north, south, east— lighted by windows placed at regular intervals; above it were wooden galleries; and above these an upper cornice, which projected so far over the area as to shelter the little tables, built of lava and covered with marble, on which the fullers and cloth-merchants exhibited their goods. The walls are divided into large panels, painted

* Sir William Gell, "Pompeiana," i. 13, *et seq.*

alternately red and yellow, and bordered at the bottom with a gay floral design; their centre is occupied by a small figure or landscape. One of the latter is described by Sir William Gell as "presenting a pretty and picturesque group of buildings, and serving to give an idea of the beautiful effects which must frequently have been produced by the various combinations of shrines, columns, and ornamental pediments in the cities of Greece and Italy." The floral decorations include a flower not unlike the lily in form, but of a vermilion colour. The effect of the whole, when fresh and new, must have been very attractive.

The chalcidicum is raised above the level of the area, and was probably approached by steps of wood; it is divided into two parts by a semicircular apse or recess, which may have served for a civil tribunal. Here, perhaps, were kept the goods not disposed of during the day.

Behind the recess, in a niche panelled in green and red, stands the statue of Eumachia, the public priestess, and foundress of the building. It is executed in white marble; is nearly 5 feet 4 inches high; and stands on a pedestal about three feet from the pavement, which bears the following inscription :—

EVMACHIÆ . L . F
SACERD . PVBL.
FVLLONES.

from which it appears that the fullers erected it to the memory of their great benefactor.

Over the side-entrance from the Strada dell' Abondanza,

may be read another inscription, explanatory of the erection of the building. It runs thus,—

> EVMACHIA . L . F . SACERD . PVBLIC . NOMINE . SVO . ET
> M . NVMISTRI . FRONTONIS . FELI . CHALCIDICVM .
> CRYPTAM . PORTICVM . CONCORDIÆ . AVGVSTÆ .
> PIETATE . SVA PEQVNIA . FECIT . EADEMQVE
> DEDICAVIT.

> [Eumachia, the public priestess, daughter of Lucius, in her own name and that of her son, M. Numistrus Fronto, erected this Chalcidicum and Crypto-Porticus at her own expense, and dedicated the same to Concord and Piety.]

This inscription was repeated on blocks of marble, which formed the architrave of the front of the building.

It has been conjectured that the chalcidicum suffered severely in the earthquake of A.D. 63; and it seems to have been undergoing repair at the time of the great eruption.

On the outer wall towards the street are two inscriptions. The first notifies a gladiatorial show,—

> A . SVETTI CERII
> ÆDILIS . FAMILIA . GLADIATORIA . PVGNABIT
> POMPEIS . R . K . JVNIAS . VENATIO . ET . VELA .
> ERVNT.

> [The gladiatorial troupe of Suettius Curius, the ædile, will fight at Pompeii on the last day of May. There will be a chase of wild beasts (*venatio*', and awnings (*vela*) to protect spectators from the sun.]

The second proves the opulence of the city,—

> C . CVSPIVM PANSAM . ÆD .
> AVRIFICES . VNIVERSI
> ROG.

> [All the goldsmiths solicit the protection of Caius Crispius Pansa the ædile].

The fullers were an important guild among the ancient Romans. Wool was then the principal material of dress, and, in so warm a climate as that of Italy, must have needed frequent purification. The fuller and the cloth manufacturer, therefore, played an important *rôle*, and we need not wonder that a building of such dimensions was appropriated to their accommodation.

But I now pass on to the so-called

TEMPLE OF QUIRINUS,

formerly known as that of Mercury. There is reason to believe, however, that if its former appellation was erroneous, its present is not correct. It was suggested by an inscription on a basis which stands in front of it, and which commemorates the achievements of Romulus, and his deification under the name of Quirinus. But it should be remembered that the said basis was not found within the temple precincts, but parallel with the colonnade of the forum; while a precisely similar pedestal, inscribed to the glory of Æneas, stood on the other side, exactly opposite to it. Hence it is evident that they anciently supported statues of the two divine founders of the Roman people.

A temple, however, the building before us is, most undoubtedly; though we know not to what deity it may have been consecrated. It occupies a roughly quadrangular area, 57½ feet by 50½ feet; at whose further extremity, elevated on a podium, or basement, stands a sacellum, or sanctuary. On each side of the basement, steps lead up to the platform of the *cella*. In front of it, and just in the centre of the court, stands a white marble altar, bearing an unfinished bas-relief, which has absurdly been supposed to represent Cicero sacrificing,—from a fancied resemblance in the principal figure to the great orator whose eloquence moved the passions of republican Rome. But if no dispassionate observer can recognize Cicero, the bas-relief is nevertheless of high interest in its details. You see the victim—an ox—led forward by the *popa*, or person whose office was to slay it. He bears in his hand the sacrificial axe (*malleus*), and is stripped naked to his waist. At the altar stands the chief priest, or perhaps magistrate, his brow bound with a triumphal wreath, and his robes partly drawn over his head. In his hand he holds a *patera*, with which to lustrate and sprinkle the victim. Behind him, carrying a vase and another patera, stands a youthful acolyte, with the sacred *vitta*, or fillet, hanging from his neck. Near him is a figure also holding a patera, which, apparently, is heaped with cakes. A musician lustily sounds a tibia or double flute, and in the rear gather the lictors with their fasces. The temple is represented in the background, adorned with garlands and festoons.

On the opposite side of the altar, young olive-trees are sculptured, and between them a crown of oak leaves, bound with the sacred *vitta*; on the other two sides, you may trace the various implements and ornaments of sacrifice, as the vase, the patera, the vitta, the censor, garlands, a ladle, and a spiral instrument, which mayhap belonged to the haruspex, who examined the entrails of the victims, and from their appearance divined the future. In fine, this altar of white marble is a curious illustration of the religious rites of antiquity, and may remind us of one which Paul beheld at Athens, dedicated to an unknown god.

The *sacellum* is built of stone, and decorated externally with pilasters; it measures but 15½ feet by 13 feet 8 inches, and was only just large enough to serve as a shrine for the statue of its presiding deity, whose pedestal is still extant. In the apartments designed for the priests numerous *amphoræ*, or wine-jars, have been discovered. These and other relics are still preserved in the temple, which has been converted into a species of temporary museum. The sounds of music no longer float through its pillared aisles; the victim no longer bleeds on its altar; the crowds of excited worshippers have ceased to bend before the marble image of their fabulous divinity; the old creed has died out, the old worship passed away; and the gods of Rome and Hellas are but as vain shadows, which the brush of the artist and the pen of the poet seek at times to recall to a transient life. They have fallen before the eternal spirit of Infinite Good.

> " The powers of earth and air
> Fled from the folding star of Bethlehem:
> Apollo, Pan, and Love,
> And even Olympian Jove,
> Grew weak, for killing truth had glared on them."

The third important building on the eastern side of the Forum is generally supposed to be

THE SENACULUM,

or Senate-House; but it has also been called the Decurionate, the meeting-place of the Town-Council, or, in

English phrase, the Guildhall. For such a purpose it seems specially adapted by its large dimensions, its spacious area measuring 83 feet by 60. It is semicircular in plan. Externally it is embellished with a portico of fluted white marble columns of the Ionic order. Internally, a niche for a statue occurs on each side of the entrance, and at the end a recess with a seat for the worshipful magistrates. An altar stands in the centre of the area, where, on important occasions, sacrifices were offered previous to the commencement of public business. It is a moot question whether the building was open to the sky, or roofed, with glass casements in the roof to admit light. Certainly, if covered, it would not be sufficiently illuminated by the rays which would stream in through the portico. It is a mistake to suppose that the ancients were not acquainted with glass windows. A quantity of flat glass has been discovered among the ruins at Pompeii; and it has also been found "ingeniously fitted" to those rare and minute openings, or loopholes, which were used as windows in that city.

We have now arrived at the north-eastern angle of the Forum, and at an edifice which has been variously designated

THE PANTHEON,

the Temple of Augustus, and the House of the Augustales.* Bonucci, an Italian archæologist of considerable repute, considers a portion of it to have served as the Temple of Augustus, and the remainder as the scene of the sacred banquet of its priests, the Augustales. Sir

* Overbeck, "Pompeji," *ut antè*; Sir W. Gell, "Pompeiana," i. 46–68.

William Gell observes that the only reason to doubt this theory is "the difficulty of finding so large a piece of ground, in the centre of a city already built, for the erection of such a fabric, and for such a purpose, at so late a period." But Vitruvius gives such a situation for the Temple of Augustus. Fragments of an inscription, too, have been found, which seem to settle the question :—

. . . AMINI . AVGVSTALI . SODALI
AVGVSTALI . Q.

And though Overbeck, apparently on no other ground than that the edifice is of a circular form, calls it the Temple of Vesta, most authorities are now agreed in accepting Bonucci's hypothesis.

The Augustales were highly honoured; they were an order founded by Augustus, and it was their privilege, like that of a chosen body of knights, to lead the troops in battle; they also presided at the feasts called Augustalia, held in memory of their founder. At Pompeii, where they were six in number, they exercised a paramount influence. Their funds supplied them with the means of giving splendid entertainments,—a source of civic popularity in other days than those of the Roman empire!—and there can be no doubt that they and the principal citizens of Pompeii often made the walls of the so-called Pantheon resound with the noise of their carousals. I can fancy that with the Pompeians it was as much a matter of eager contention to obtain an invitation to a *cæna* with the Augustales, as it is with a certain class of Londoners now-a-days to partake of the turtle-soup of the Mansion-House! *Nunc pellite curas!*

O Pompeians, let us drink and be merry, for what says our Horace?

> "Sapias, vina liques, et spatio brevi
> Spem longam reseces."

> "Be wise; pour forth the wine:
> Within one narrow span thy wandering hopes confine."

It is, at all events, certain that feasting was the principal motive for assembling in the Pompeian porticoes. The street which runs along the north side of them from the Temple of Jupiter has been called that of *Dried Fruits*, from the quantity of raisins, figs, plums, chestnuts, preserved fruits in glass vases, lentils, hempseed, and similar articles, found in the shops. Bread, scales, money, and moulds for pastry, have also been among the "treasure-trove;" and a finely-wrought statuette of Fame, in bronze, with golden armlets.

Many of the smaller paintings which adorned the walls of the building are of a culinary character. At the northern entrance, which has the name CELSVM engraved on a pilaster, and near which was found a box containing a gold ring, 41 silver medals, and 1036 brass coins, you may see a group of Cupids making bread, or driving the patient ass, crowned with a wreath—like Bottom in the "Midsummer Night's Dream," after his metamorphosis—which brought the flour. On the opposite side, their dexterous fingers are weaving garlands for the guests. At the southern entrance a tableau is made up of a meat-axe, boars' heads, hams, fish, and other viands. In other places we find paintings of geese, turkeys, dishes of eggs, fowls and game plucked ready for cooking, oxen, sheep, glass salvers of fruit, a cornucopia, a variety of amphoræ for wine, and every other accessory of a banquet. The Augustales must have shown considerable taste in drawing up their bills of fare.

To this pictorial evidence may be added the testimony of a drain or sink near the tholos or dodecagon in the centre of the court, which was found obstructed with fish-bones and other remains of food.

The Pantheon was a spacious edifice, consisting internally of an open *atrium* or court, 120 feet by 90 feet, with entrances on three sides; that from the Forum being decorated with fluted Corinthian columns of white marble, and pedestals for statues. The columns had been overthrown by the earthquake, and were under repair at the time of the eruption. In the atrium was placed an altar, surrounded by twelve small pedestals. It was originally supposed that these had borne statues of the twelve *Dii Consentes* or *Magni*—Jupiter, Juno, Minerva, Vesta, Ceres, Neptune, Venus, Vulcan, Mars, Mercury, Apollo, Diana; and therefore the building was named the Pantheon. It is more probable, as Overbeck suggests,[*] that they supported some light wooden structure—perhaps a canopy for the protection of the officiating priests—which was destroyed in the fire that consumed the city.

Behind the altar was a niche, in which may have been placed the image of a god, so that the devout Roman had an opportunity of leaving his offering as he entered, and of propitiating the presiding deity.

The grand entrance from the Forum opens out of the portico north of the Senaculum, and has two doors, be-

[*] Overbeck, " Pompeji," *ut ant*.

tween which stood a statue—probably of the Emperor—under a pediment supported by two small Corinthian columns of white marble, whose capitals are enriched with foliage and the Roman eagles.

On the left of this entrance the wall, with its paintings, has been excellently preserved; and when it was fresh, nothing could exceed the beauty of the colouring, or the

STATUES OF LIVIA AND DRUSUS, FOUND IN THE PANTHEON.

rich effect of the contrast between its many vivid tints and the deep black of the panelled background. The finest frescoes are those of Ulysses and Penelope, Theseus and Æthra, and the muse Thalia.

In the first, reference is made to the passage in the 19th book of the Odyssey, where Penelope inquires of the supposed mendicant—who is Ulysses himself—for tidings of the lost Ulysses. She is clothed in a violet-coloured tunic and white veil, with materials for spinning in her hand. Ulysses, who is seated, wears a white tunic, and a yellow chlamys. Eurynome, the attendant, is seen in the background. The expression and attitude of the figures are admirable.

> " Thus the famed hero, perfected in wiles,
> With fair similitudes of truth beguiles
> The queen's attentive ear: dissolved in woe,
> From the bright eyes the tears unbounded flow.
> As snows collected on the mountain freeze,
> When milder regions breathe a vernal breeze,
> The fleecy pile obeys the whispering gales,
> Ends in a stream, and murmurs through the vales:
> So, melted with the pleasing tale he told,
> Down the fair cheek the copious torrent rolled:
> She to her present lord laments him lost,
> And views that object which she wants the most!":*

Of the next picture the subject seems to have been taken from the story of Theseus, and to represent his discovery of his father's sword by raising the enormous rock under which it lay concealed. His mother Æthra sits near, and seems explaining the circumstances to Theseus, whose strength had thus been proved in accordance with the injunctions of his father Ægeus. But the picture has suffered greatly from exposure, and many antiquarians contend that it really represents Mercury restoring Io to liberty, after having slain her custodian Argus with the sword which he holds in his hand.

Very beautiful in conception and execution is the picture of Thalia, who, crowned with a golden tiara, is represented seated ; a *pedum* or hooked stick in one hand,

* Homer, " The Odyssey," book xix., translation by Pope.

and a mask and wreath in the other. A drum or tympanum is placed by her side, and a graceful female, perhaps a sister muse, leans upon the back of her chair.

Another striking design represents an architectural composition set between two of the black panels already described. Over a richly ornamented portico, seen through a graceful arch, hangs a pergula or trellis-work of vines. On the right stands a group of Doric columns. Through the opening approaches the figure of the paintress herself, carrying her palette. The little pediments of the shrines on each side are very elegant, and beneath them are pictures of Roman galleys, brightly painted. In a lower compartment, which forms a species of base or substruction, is a female figure with a lyre. The whole glows vividly with bright vermilion, emerald green, deep crimson, golden yellow, and azure blue, while the architecture in the background is tinted with the aerial purple of distance. The general effect is very bright and vivacious.

That this edifice, so radiantly enriched with design and colour, was intended to accommodate a large number of guests, may be inferred from the very considerable depth of the porticoes,* being 24 feet on the western side. They must have been roofed with timber, and have sloped inwards to the court, where the rain-water was received in a large channel. It is possible that only the southern, western, and northern sides had porticoes, and that the eastern was left open towards the temple to admit light.

On the south lies a range of eleven small chambers—

* Sir W. Gell, "Pompeiara," i. 57.

each about 10 feet by 8—which appear to have been used, like the recesses in a modern restaurant, for the separate repasts of private parties. They are all painted in red panels.

Above them was a second story, as is evident from the joists which supported the upper floor, and the painted walls of the higher rooms. They would seem to have been approached by an external staircase, and a long narrow gallery. These upper chambers were probably called *Cænacula*, which, we know, were always placed in the upper story of a Roman house. Here were low circular tables of fir-wood or maple, or occasionally of citron-wood, plated with silver, and supported on legs of ivory. They were covered by draperies of wool or silk, embroidered or striped with gold or purple; and around them were arranged the *triclinia* (*tres lecti*, τρεις κλιναι, three couches) for the accommodation of the guests who did not sit at table, but reclined. Three commonly rested on each couch. They lay with the upper part of the body resting on the left arm, the head a little raised, the back supported by cushions, and the limbs either slightly bent or stretched out at full length. The feet of the first came behind the back of the second, and *his* feet behind the back of the third. A cushion was placed between each guest.

The *cæna* or dinner of the Romans consisted of two divisions, called *Mensa prima*, the first course—different kinds of meat; and *Mensa secunda vel altera*, the second course—fruits and sweets. In later times the first part was called *Gustatio* or *Gustus*, and composed of such dishes as might stimulate the appetite; for example, oysters, eggs, asparagus, lettuce, onions, figs, and a *mulsum* of wine mingled with water and sweetened with honey. Then came a plentiful supply of fish—mullet, lamprey, sturgeon, pike, and turbot; and for meat, a peacock, a pheasant, a kid, a guinea-hen, ducks, geese, nightingales, thrushes, and perhaps a whole boar stuffed with the flesh of other animals. To wash down this abundant banquet wines were served up, either mixed with water or with spices, and drunk either hot or cold.

Some idea of a Roman cæna may be obtained from the following passages in Juvenal:—*

> "See! by the tallest servant borne on high,
> A sturgeon fills the largest dish and eye!
> With how much pomp he's placed upon the board!
> With what a tail and breast salutes his lord
> With what expense and art, how richly drest,
> Garnished with 'sparagus, himself a feast!....
>   Behold a mullet even from Corfu brought,
> Or near the rocks of Taurominium caught.....
>   The largest lamprey which their seas afford,
> Is made a sacrifice to Virro's board.....
>   Near him is placed the liver of a goose,
> That part alone which luxury would choose.
> A boar entire, and worthy of the sword
> Of Meleager, smokes upon the board.
> Next mushrooms, larger when the clouds descend
> In fruitful showers, and desired thunders rend
> The vernal air.....
>   If the blood boil, and the adventitious fire
> Raised by high meats, and higher wines, require
> To temper and allay the burning heat,
> Waters are brought, which by decoction get
> New coolness, such plain nature does not know,
> Not ice so cool, nor hyperborean snow."

The dishes of the second course, or dessert, were called *bellaria*, and included apples, pears, nuts, figs, olives,

---
* Juvenal, "Satire" v., translated by Bowles (Dryden's edition of Juvenal).

grapes; *pistachia*, or pistachio nuts; *caricæ*, or dried figs; *uvæ passæ*, dried grapes, or raisins; *dactyli*, dates; *boleti*, mushrooms; *nuclei*, or pine-nut kernels; and sweetmeats or confections, called *edulia mellita, cupediæ, crustula, liba, placentæ, coptæ*, almond-cakes, *artologani* or cheese-cakes, and *scriblitæ*, or cakes.

Such was the kind of entertainment to which the Augustales would invite their fellow-citizens.

The open court, or atrium, is paved with pebbles imbedded in a species of hard cement. In the centre stood a *tholos* or dodecagonal building, consisting of a roof supported by twelve piers. It was paved with marble, and from the situation and substance of the piers we may conclude that the roof was framed of light timbers meeting in an apex in the centre, and with projecting eaves. At the north-eastern angle a projection from the wall has been supposed by lively imaginations to be an orchestra, a bar for distributing wines and liquors, and a money-taker's office! The truth is, that no one has the slightest idea of its exact uses, and modern customs suggest a modern appropriation.

Beyond this, and forming the angle of the building, lies an apartment or enclosure about 35 feet long, and nearly of the same breadth, decorated with many frescoes now defaced. Here also is a sacellum, which has had its statue and its altar, and is likewise embellished with mural paintings, representing sea-horses and griffins, dogs hunting stags, and a lioness chasing two bulls.

The centre of the eastern side was occupied by the temple, while the other angle includes a chamber whose uses it is difficult to understand, unless it was a refreshment-room. A species of table runs round three sides of it, at a distance of about 3 feet from the northern and eastern, and 9 feet from the southern walls, leaving an open area in the centre of about 30 feet. The table or bench is about 3 feet wide. It inclines from the walls outward, and a channel beneath is arranged to catch whatever fell from its sloping surface.

I suppose this table was used by the Augustales or their cooks when cutting up victims for the sacrifice, or carving viands for the feast. Or it may have supported rows of bottles of those beverages, warm and iced, which the Pompeians so largely delighted in; and vases and dishes of "honied sweets," lucent syrups, and dainty cates. Snow, or rather ice, was much employed by the Romans in cooling water, and the iced water they mixed with their Falernian and Massic wines. And sometimes they tempered the "indomitum Falernium" of Pusius, or the Setinum, which Silius Italicus declares so choice as to be reserved for the God of Wine himself—

"Ipsius mensis reposta Lyæi"—

by passing it through a strainer partly filled with snow. Is there anything new under the sun—at least, in the way of luxurious living? The modern epicure, who ices his wines, does but reproduce the practice of a Pompeian *gourmand*. Ever flourishing seems that vain epicurean philosophy, "Vivamus, dum licet esse bene."

I now come to the temple, which occupies the central division on the eastern side of the edifice, and is approached by a flight of steps within its vestibule or pronaos. On the wall of this same pronaos is painted a sitting figure, which some authorities represent to be Augustus, but is rather a Bacchanal, with a thyrsus in one hand, and a dish of fruits in the other. A statue of the great Emperor probably stood on a pedestal without the entrance, as a hand grasping a globe was found near the spot. Livia and Drusus was found, at the time of the excavations, in the right and left niches. The walls were probably painted.

Thus have we completed our survey of the misnamed Pantheon,—of the halls and chambers which, two thousand years ago, echoed with the sound of laughter and merriment, and are now silent as the grave. Of all the feasting and the revelry, what remains? Where be now the jibes and jĕsts, the toast to the reigning beauty, the arrowy epigram, the subtle allusion? Nowhere, perhaps, so keenly as in Pompeii do we understand the full and pregnant meaning of the Preacher's "Vanitas Vanitatum." Not even at Nineveh or Heliopolis, among the marble ruins of Tadmor, or the wondrous colossal effigies of El Karnak, is the sad truth so powerfully obtruded upon us. For there everything is desolate—everything tells of a remote decay and spoliation—and we regard it with the curiosity of the antiquarian, poring for a name, or a date, or a chance light to be thrown upon the dark passages of history; but at Pompeii the banquet-hall and the bedchamber, the theatre and the forum, seem so near to us, and so linked with ourselves in our tastes and feelings and objects, that we start at their eloquent evidences of mutability! They cry aloud to us with a voice which we cannot but choose to hearken. They flaunt in our faces the constant testimony of our follies. Build, and strive, and labour, and destroy; drink, and eat, and sleep; but upon all that you do, and all that you leave undone, *we* supply the commentary. It is the same now as yesterday—*Vanitas Vanitatum!*

Such, at least, is the lesson, ever trite and ever true, which I read in the silence and the solitude of the Buried City.

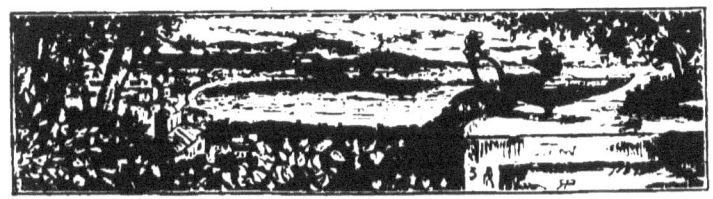

IV.

The Temple of Fortune.

" The old Scythians
Painted blind Fortune's powerful hands with wings,
To show her gifts come swift and suddenly,
Which, if her favourite be not swift to take,
He loses them for ever."
                                    GEORGE CHAPMAN.

HE next public building to which I propose the reader should accompany me is situated in the Street of Fortune—a continuation of the Street of Mercuries—and is named the Temple of Fortune. It may be considered, says no mean authority,* one of the best examples of the Roman style now extant, and is doubly interesting, as being the erection of the Tullian family, immortalized in the person of Cicero.

Before describing it, I may inform my younger readers that the places consecrated by the Romans to the worship of their gods were called *Templa*, or temples. A small temple or chapel, generally attached to some longer building, was a *sacellum* or an *ædicula*. The place erected for offering sacrifices was named *ara* or *altare;* the secret chamber, to which none but the priests were admitted,

* Sir W. Gell, " Pompeiana," i. 69, *et seq*.

adytum. The body of the temple, answering to the nave of a modern church, the Romans called the *cella;* it was approached through the *pronaos,* or vestibule.

TEMPLE OF FORTUNE RESTORED.

The Temple of Fortune is placed cornerwise to the street, with its portico turned a little towards the Forum, and stands upon an elevated *podium* or basement, about

THE PORTICO AND CELLA.

eight feet high, built with good blocks of travertine. It had two entrances of three steps each, separated by a projecting platform, which may have supported a statue, or, more probably, the altar where blazed the incense and sacrifices of the numerous votaries of the fickle goddess—

"Fortune, the great commandress of the world."

The iron rails which prevented the entrance of the profane are yet visible in front of this platform, and were passed by two gates, each 5 palms 4 inches wide, placed on the lower platform after an ascent of four steps. From the platform, which extended the whole width of the temple, you ascended by a flight of eight steps to the portico, and its eight Corinthian columns of white marble. The whole building was *veneered*, so to speak, both without and within, with thin slabs of the same material. The cornice and mouldings were richly carved with floral and other devices.

From the portico, or pronaos, you entered the cella, decorated externally with five pilasters on each side. It measured about 33 feet 8 inches in length. At its extremity was a semicircular recess, containing a small Corinthian ædicula or shrine, richly finished and designed; and within the ædicula stood of old a statue of the goddess. The recess was 14 feet 2 inches wide; the shrine, 9 feet 4 inches.

On the marble architrave of the shrine may be seen the following inscription :

M . TVLLIVS . M . F . D . V . I . D . TER . QVINQ . AVGVR . TV . MIL
A . POP . ÆDEM . FORTVNÆ . AVGVST . SOLO . ET . PEG . SVA.

That is: Marcus Tullius, the Duumvir, thrice elected Augur by the people, erected this temple to Fortuna Augusta on his own soil and at his own charge. It is generally believed that he was a descendant of the great orator who first made the Tullian family renowned. A statue, of life-size, found in the interior of the building, is described as having borne some resemblance to the authentic busts of Cicero. He was represented clothed in the toga prætexta, or official robe of the Roman magistrates; and, which renders the statue of peculiar interest, this robe was entirely painted of the costly imperial dye —a deep purple violet. Hence it is believed that the prætexta, instead of being a garment with only a purple hem, was dyed throughout of this famous hue. Its cost was enormous; the violet, though the less precious kind, was valued, according to Pliny, at 100 denarii, or £3, 4s. 7d. the pound; the red (*rubra Tarentina*) at 1000 denarii, or ten times that amount. It was obtained from a shell-fish called the *murex*. The species producing the violet dye was found near Tarentum; the red was chiefly brought from the neighbourhood of Tyre. The Roman "purple" has passed into our poetry to express any radiance of indescribable beauty, as Gray speaks of

"The bloom of young desire and purple light of love."

Within the cella was also found a female statue, life-size, clothed in a tunic falling to her feet, and a toga over it. The face has been sawn off; apparently from economy, as if the Pompeians, desirous of complimenting some distinguished personage, had thought the cheapest way to do so was by substituting her face for that originally belonging to the statue.

In the area privata, on the south side of the temple, vestiges may be discerned of what seem to have been the priests' offices. At the end near the altar is a hole, which probably served to facilitate the mysteries of responses or oracles. The ancient priests must have been expert jugglers; and it is certain they were acquainted with many of the acoustical and optical deceptions which are the stock-in-trade of the modern thaumaturgist.

The street running from the Temple to the Forum is now called the Street of Fortune. A rich harvest of discovery has at various times been discovered here. The curious reader may consult the pages of Overbeck for elaborate details of glass bottles, statues, bronze statuettes, bronze lamps and stands, vases, gold earrings, basins, pateræ, bells,

SPECIMEN OF MARBLES FOUND AT POMPEII.

lamps, coins, weights and scales, dishes of clay and terra cotta, glazed plates, and other memorials of a remote antiquity. They are not so much valuable in themselves, as of interest from the light which they throw upon the manners and customs of a past age, and the commentary they furnish on the writings of the Latin classics.

The skeleton was also found here of a Pompeian, who, apparently for the sake of sixty coins, a small plate and a saucepan of silver, had delayed in his house till the street was already half filled with volcanic matter. He would seem to have been in the act of escaping from his window, when death suddenly cut short his career.

V.

The Amphitheatres.

"This the crowd surveys
Oft in the theatre, whose awnings broad,
Bedecked with crimson, yellow, or the tint
Of steel cerulean, from their fluted heights
Wave tremulous; and o'er the scene beneath,
Each marble statue, and the rising rows
Of rank and beauty, fling their tint superb;
While as the walls with ampler shade repel
The garish noon-beam, every object round
Laughs with a deeper dye, and wears profuse
A lovelier lustre, ravished from the day."
                    LUCRETIUS, iv. 73 (*Translation by Mason Good*).

HE Romans borrowed most of their amusements from the Greeks; and that which they did not borrow*—the *ludi amphitheatrales*, the exhibition of combats of gladiators and wild beasts—was marked by the innate cruelty and barbaric love of excitement peculiar to the Roman character. The refined genius of the Greek shrank from the fierce amusement to be obtained in watching the death-struggles of the hired athletes. Dearer to him the contention in the chariot race, or the wrestle, or the recitation of melodious song. He loved whatever appealed to his

---

* It is said that gladiatorial combats were first introduced by the Etruscans; but the shows of the amphitheatre were, nevertheless, characteristically Roman.

imagination, whatever cherished his passion for the ideal. Such joys were tame to the ruder and harsher Roman: his blood could only be fired by exhibitions of physical prowess or physical suffering. So when the slave perished in a lion's jaws, or the retiarius sank beneath the deadly blows of the secutor, his eyes flashed and his heart thrilled: he had no pity for the victim, while he bestowed his loudest applause on the victor.

Gladiators were first exhibited at Rome in B.C. 264, on the occasion of the funeral rites of the elder Brutus. For some years they were confined to public funerals, but afterwards they fought at most funerals of any importance, and even at those of women. They were also exhibited at entertainments and public festivals, to please the people. The appetite grew by what it fed on, and these cruel displays became in time a necessary feature of every great popular show. Wealthy and ambitious individuals vied with each other who should exhibit the most imposing spectacles. The numbers engaged in them were almost incredible. After Trajan's victory over the Dacians, and his consequent triumph, not less than ten thousand gladiators fought in the Flavian amphitheatre.

The men who thus perilled life and limb "to make a Roman's holiday" were either captives, slaves, condemned criminals, or free-born citizens who fought for hire. Of the criminals some were said to be condemned *ad gladium*, which gave them a twelvemonth's respite; others *ad ludum*, and these might attain their discharge at the expiration of three years. Freemen who voluntarily assumed the gladiator's sword were called *auctorati*.

In the more licentious days of the empire even equites and senators descended into the arena, and women whom vice and luxury had unsexed ; but the latter practice was prohibited by Severus.

Schools (*ludi*) of gladiators were kept by persons called *lanistæ*, who either let them out to persons desirous of gaining popularity by a gladiatorial show, or trained them—as horses are now-a-days trained—for some wealthy citizen. The curriculum which they underwent appears to have been as carefully considered as the training of a modern prize-fighter.

There were various classes of gladiators, distinguished by their arms, different mode of fighting, or other circumstances. Thus :

The *andabatæ* fought blindfold, their helmets having no apertures for the eyes ; and consequently their various manœuvres, and blows delivered on the empty air, proved highly amusing to the spectators.

The *dimacheri* were so called because they fought with two swords.

The *equites* fought on horseback ; the *essedarii* from chariots, like the Gauls and Britons.

The *hoplomachi* appeared in a full suit of armour.

The *laqueatores* were those who employed a noose or lasso to entangle their opponents.

The *mirmillones* were so called, it is said, because they bore on their helmets the figure of a fish (*mormyr*, μορμύρος) —in allusion, perhaps, to their nimbleness. Their arms being like those of the Gauls, they were frequently named *Galli*. They were generally pitted against the retiarii, or Thracians.

The *retiarii*, for their only weapon, carried a three-pointed lance (*tridens* or *fuscina*); but they also bore a net (*rete*), which they endeavoured to fling over their antagonists, and then, while they were thus embarrassed, they attacked them with the fuscina. But if they missed their aim in throwing the net, they were liable, while preparing for another cast, to be struck down by the secutores or mirmillones, with whom they usually fought.

The *secutores* were probably so named because, in their combats with the retiarii, they pursued the latter when the throw of the net had failed.

The gladiatorial shows began with a kind of sham battle—a *prælusio*, or prelude—fought with wooden swords, or laths. Then the trumpet sounded, and the bloody battle began. A *venatio*, or combat with wild beasts, formed one of the earliest portions of the entertainment. Either the wild beasts fought with one another, or with men. The Romans had a passion almost amounting to madness for these sanguinary scenes, and thousands of animals were slain in one sanguinary day. One of the earliest venationes was that exhibited by Marcus Fulvius in B.C. 186, when lions and panthers were let loose against each other. A hundred lions were exhibited by Sulla in his prætorship, and destroyed by skilful javelin men sent by King Bocchus for the purpose. At a venatio celebrated by Pompey in his second consulship, B.C. 55, six hundred lions were slaughtered, and eighteen or twenty elephants. Bull-fights were introduced by Julius Cæsar; and Augustus brought into the arena six-and-thirty crocodiles.* At the consecration of the great amphitheatre by Titus, five thousand wild and four thousand tame animals were slain—a slaughter which might have sickened the greediest Roman of blood. But in the games celebrated by Trajan after his Dacian wars, no less than eleven thousand animals were butchered. "Under the emperors," says a writer already quoted, "we read of a particular kind of venatio, in which the beasts were not killed by *bestiarii* (gladiators so called, trained to contend with wild beasts), but were given up to the people, who were allowed to rush into the area of the circus and carry away what they pleased. On such occasions a number of large trees, which had been torn up by the roots, was planted in the circus, which thus resembled a forest, and none of the more savage animals were admitted into it. A venatio of this kind was exhibited by the elder Gordian in his ædileship, and a painting of the forest with the animals in it is described by Julius Capitolinus. One of the most extraordinary venationes of this kind was that given by Probus, in which there were a thousand ostriches, a thousand stags, a thousand boars, a thousand deer, and numbers of wild goats, wild sheep, and other animals of the same kind. The more savage animals were slain by the bestiarii in the amphitheatre—a hundred lions, and the same number of lionesses, a hundred Libyan and a hundred Syrian leopards, and three hundred bears. It is unnecessary to multiply examples, as the above are sufficient to give an idea of the numbers and variety of animals at these spectacles; but the list of beasts which

* Dion Cassius, quoted in Dr. Smith's "Dictionary of Antiquities," article *Venatio*.

were collected by the younger Gordian for his triumph, and exhibited by his successor Philip at the secular games, deserve mention on account of their variety and the rarity of some of them. Among them we find mention of thirty-two elephants, ten elks, ten tigers (which seem to have been very seldom exhibited), sixty tame lions, thirty tame leopards, ten hyænas, an hippopotamus and rhinoceros, ten archohontes (it is unknown what they were), ten camelopards, twenty anagri (wild asses, or perhaps zebras), forty wild horses, and an immense number of similar animals."

These exhibitions originally took place in the forum and the circus; the gladiatorial displays in the former, and the shows of wild beasts in the latter. But as neither was well adapted for such purposes, a new form of building became requisite, in which a multitude of spectators should be so accommodated that all might obtain a good view of the area occupied by the combatants; while the area required to be of quite a distinct shape to the circus, inasmuch as the combatants were to be confined as much as possible in the same place. Accordingly the amphitheatre was designed, the idea being suggested by the existing theatre. In fact, the first amphitheatre—that of C. Scribonius Curio—was simply a double theatre (ἀμφί and θέατρον), or two movable theatres, which could be placed face to face, or back to back, according to the species of entertainment to be celebrated. The next amphitheatre, and apparently the first to which the name was applied, was built by Julius Cæsar in B.C. 46, and built of wood. The first permanent amphitheatre, partly of stone and partly of wood, was erected by Statilius

Taurus, at the instigation of Augustus, who well understood the political value of public shows and festivals as a means of amusing the people. This was burned down in the reign of Nero, and, though restored, did not satisfy the magnificent ideas of Vespasian, who commenced the gigantic pile, completed by Titus, which, under the name of the Coliseum, has obtained a worldwide celebrity, and whose mighty ruins still command the admiration of the stranger.

> "The gladiators' bloody circus stands,
> A noble wreck in ruinous perfection ;
> While Cæsar's chambers and the Augustan halls
> Grovel on earth in indistinct decay."

Externally the amphitheatre generally consisted of an oval wall, composed of two or more stories of arcades, supported by piers of different architectural orders, adorned with pilasters or attached pillars. Within, an equal number of tiers of galleries (*maeniana*) gave access to the spectators at different elevations. But a better idea of this interior may be obtained from Gibbon's matchless description of the Roman Coliseum than from any elaborate architectural statement.

"The slopes," he says,* "of the vast concave which formed the inside were filled and surrounded with sixty or eighty rows of marble seats, covered with cushions, and capable of receiving with ease about 80,000 spectators. Sixty-four *vomitories* (for by that name the doors were very aptly distinguished) poured forth the immense multitude ; and the entrances, passages, and staircases were contrived with such exquisite skill that each person,

* Gibbon, "Decline and Fall of the Roman Empire."

whether of the senatorial, the equestrian, or the plebeian order, arrived at his destined place without trouble or confusion. Nothing was omitted which, in any respect, could be subservient to the convenience and pleasure of the spectators. They were protected from the sun and rain by an ample canopy, occasionally drawn over their heads. The air was continually refreshed by the playing of fountains, and profusely impregnated by the grateful scent of aromatics.* In the centre of the edifice the *arena* or stage was strewed with the finest sand, and successively assumed the most different forms. At one moment it seemed to rise out of the earth, like the garden of the Hesperides, and was afterwards broken into the rocks and caverns of Thrace. The subterraneous pipes conveyed an inexhaustible supply of water; and what had just before appeared a level plain, might be suddenly converted into a wide lake, covered with armed vessels, and replenished with the monsters of the deep. In the decoration of these scenes the Roman emperors displayed their wealth and liberality; and we read on various occasions that the whole furniture of the amphitheatre consisted either of silver, or of gold, or of amber. The poet who describes the games of Carinus, in the character of a shepherd attracted to the capital by the

---

* To this Lucan alludes in the following passage :—

> ". . As when mighty Rome's spectators meet
> In the full theatre's capacious seat,
> At once, by secret pipes and channels fed,
> Rich tinctures gush from every antique head ;
> At once ten thousand saffron currents flow,
> And rain their odours on the crowd below."
>
> *Pharsalia*, book ix.

fame of their magnificence, affirms that the nets designed as a defence against the wild beasts were of gold wire, that the porticoes were gilded, and that the *belt* or circle which divided the several ranks of spectators from each other was studded with a beautiful mosaic of precious stones."

For the greater security of the spectators, trenches, called *euripi*, surrounded the arena. These were first dug by Cæsar as a protection against the elephants which he exhibited, that animal being supposed to be particularly afraid of water.

In the centre of the arena stood an altar, dedicated sometimes to Diana or Pluto, but more commonly to Jupiter Latiaris, the patron-god of Latium, in whose honour human sacrifices were offered. From certain passages in ancient writers it has been inferred, but on no satisfactory evidence, that the games of the amphitheatre were usually inaugurated by the sacrifice of a bestiarius to this sanguinary deity. Dens were constructed beneath the arena for the reception of wild beasts; and conduits provided for its inundation when it was required to be transformed into a lake, where *naumachia* or sham sea-fights might be exhibited.

With respect to the spectators, the same order of precedence was observed as at the theatre; their appropriate place being reserved for senators, equites, and plebeians. It was not a question, as with us, of money, but of rank. The *podium* was set apart for the senators; this was a broad cushioned platform which ran immediately round the arena. A covered or canopied seat was here given up to the emperor, or his representative; and it is supposed that in this part of the building were also places of honour for the exhibitor of the games and the Vestal Virgins. The equites sat in fourteen rows behind the senators, and with them the civil and military tribunes. Behind were the *popularia*, or seats of the plebeians, divided by passages (*scalæ*) into wedge-shaped compartments called *cunei*. The general superintendence of the amphitheatre was intrusted to an officer named *villicus amphitheatri*, and the distribution of the people in their proper seats to *locarii*.

A week or so before the day appointed for a gladiatorial show, he who gave it (the *editor*) caused bills or pictorial representations to be affixed to the public walls, containing the names and badges of the combatants, and stating how many would fight, and for how long a period. When the day came, the gladiators marched in procession to the amphitheatre. When a gladiator was wounded, the excited populace would shout, "*Habet!*" (He has it.) He then lowered his arms in token of submission, but his fate rested with the spectators, and not with his antagonist. If he had fought gallantly, they would press down their thumbs, and his life was saved; if they were dissatisfied, they turned up their thumbs (pollicem vertebant), and he was doomed to the sword.

> " Influenced by the rabble's bloody will,
> With thumbs bent back, they popularly kill." *

The unfortunate victim sometimes submitted to his fate with so calm an intrepidity that the people would relent at the last moment, and grant him his life. But this was only when their blood had not been heated by

* Juvenal, "Satires," iii. 36.

a series of exciting combats. Timidity, and want of courage, were of such rare occurrence, that Cicero proposes the high principle of honour which inspired the common gladiator as an admirable model of heroic constancy to animate himself and his friends in enduring all things on behalf of the commonwealth.

The bodies of the slain were dragged by a hook—*unco trahebantur*—through a gate appropriately named *Libitenensis*, the Gate of Death, to a den called the *Spoliarium*. The victors were rewarded with a sum of money, a palm-branch, and a crown of palm gaily ornamented with coloured ribbons. To those who had served three years a wooden sword, *rudis*, was presented, as a sign that he was released from the arena; and occasionally a gladiator who displayed remarkable courage or skill was enfranchised on the spot. He was then called *rudiarius*, and offered up his arms in the Temple of Hercules.*

Certain bas-reliefs discovered upon a tomb at Pompeii exhibit, in a very striking manner, the two main divisions of the gladiatorial spectacles—the *venationes*, and the combats between man and man.

This tomb is situated in the Street of Tombs, without the Gate of Herculaneum, and consists of a square chamber, serving as a basement, surmounted by three steps, upon which, and upon the uppermost part of the basement, are placed the bas-reliefs. The whole is sur-

* Horace, " Epistles," i. 1.—If a person was free before he entered the ludus, he became on his discharge free again; or if he had been a slave, he returned to slavery. A man who had been a gladiator was considered permanently disgraced, and even if he acquired wealth could not obtain the equestrian rank.— *Dictionary of Antiquities*, art. " *Gladiatores.*"

mounted by a square cippus, or funereal pillar, bearing
the following inscription :—

PATRICIO . A. F. MEN
SCAVRO
II VIR. I. D.
. . . ECVRIONES . LOCVM . MONVM .
∞ ∞ ∞ IN FVNERE ET. STATVAM EQVESTᵀR.
. . . ORO . PONENDAM . CENSVERVNT .
SCAVRVS . PATER . FILIO .

[To Patricius Scaurus, son of Aulus, of the tribe Menenia, Duumvir of Justice, by command of the decurions. The decurions decreed the site of the monument, three thousand sesterces for funeral expenses, and an equestrian statue in the Forum. Scaurus the father to his son.]

From the nature of the bas-relief one would suppose that this Patricius Scaurus had been renowned for his gladiatorial spectacles. . In one of them is given a representation of the *venatio;* a man naked and unarmed between a lion and a panther, which dart away from him in different directions. In the second, a wild boar seems dashing furiously against another naked and defenceless combatant, who in a half-recumbent posture seems prepared to spring at his enemy. The archæologist Mazois supposes that these figures belonged to a class of bestiarii who, trusting solely in their active limbs and ready minds, entered the arena merely to provoke the wild beasts after they had been let loose. In continuation of the same relief, we see a wolf at full speed, gnawing a javelin which is buried deeply in his chest; and a stag, with a rope attached to his horns, pulled down by a couple of dogs.

In the next group we may trace some steps of the training by which the bestiarius was fitted for his dangerous profession. A youth, his legs and thighs protected by cuisses, and with a javelin in each hand, attacks a panther, whose movements, however, are fettered by a rope fastened round its neck, and at the other end to a broad band passing round the body of a bull. This arrangement affords the tyro some slight protection, and yet demands his utmost wariness and agility, as the beast is still at liberty to pursue him from point to point. Behind the bull is another figure—that perhaps of the *lanista* or trainer, who goads the bull forward with a lance.

We see in another bas-relief a man contending with a bear, exactly after the fashion of the matador in the Spanish bull-fights. In one hand he carries a short sword, in the other a veil with which to baffle his adversary. As this mode of equipment was not introduced into the Roman arena until the reign of Claudius, we may infer from it the date at which the tomb was erected. Claudius became emperor in A.D. 41. In A.D. 59 theatrical exhibitions were prohibited at Pompeii for ten years. In A.D. 63 occurred the earthquake by which the monument was evidently injured. It was therefore raised between A.D. 42 and A.D. 59.*

The upper range of sculptures is devoted to gladiatorial combats. The names of the combatants are given, the number of their victories, and the name of their *lanista* or owner, one Ampliatus. On this substruction of fact Lord Lytton, in his "Last Days of Pompeii," has raised an agreeable edifice of fiction, and by introducing the actual characters immortalized on these bas-reliefs, has given to his romance a particular air of *vraisemblance.*

* Overbeck, "Pompeji," i. 179.

There are eight pairs of gladiators. The first pair, on the left, represents an equestrian combat between Bebrix, evidently from his name a foreigner, and Nobilior. Resembling much the knights of the feudal days, they bear lances and round shields (*parma*), beautifully inlaid; their armour is dexterously woven with bands of iron, but covers only the thighs and the right arms; short cloaks (*inducula*), extending to the seat, enhance the picturesque character of their costume; their legs are naked with the exception of sandals fastened a little above the ankles; and on their heads they carry iron helmets, with vizors which protected the whole face. Mounted on light and nimble steeds, we may fancy them curvetting and caracoling round the arena amid the applauding shouts of twenty thousand spectators. And now, at a given signal, they rush impetuously at one another, each advancing his round buckler, each brandishing on high his light but sturdy lance. When within a few paces of his opponent, Bebrix suddenly checks his steed in full career, wheels round, and as Nobilior sweeps by, spurs full upon him. The shield of Nobilior, skilfully and promptly put forward, receives the spear which would otherwise have drained his life-blood. Bebrix in his turn assumes the defensive; but, we may fancy, too late; Nobilior's lance seems quivering at his helmet; he raises his buckler to protect himself; but Nobilior suddenly lowering his weapon, hurls him from his horse—dead!

The group next in succession depicts two gladiators whose names are defaced. The first wears a richly ornamented helmet, with a vizor, carries the long buckler (*scutum*), and, we may presume, a sword; but the sculptor has either forgotten to represent it, or intended it to be of metal. Like all the other gladiators, he wears the *subligaculum*, a short apron of red or white stuff fastened above the hips by a girdle of bronze or embroidered leather. The right leg is cased in a coloured leather buskin, the left in an *ocrea* or greave not reaching to the knee. His antagonist is armed with a helmet ornamented with wings, a smaller buckler, thigh-pieces formed of plates of

COMBAT BETWEEN A VELES AND A SAMNITE.

iron, and on each leg the high greave which the Greeks called κνημίς. These figures appear to represent one of the light-armed class called *Veles*, and a Samnite (*Samnis*), so named because armed after the old Samnite fashion.*
The former, who has been sixteen times a conqueror in former games, is now himself conquered,—

"The desolator desolate,
The victor overthrown."

* "Pompeii" (Library of Entertaining Knowledge), i. 308.

A THRACIAN AND A MIRMILLO.

Wounded in the breast, he has let fall his buckler in token of defeat, and at the same time he solicits the pity of the spectators in the usual manner, by raising his finger towards them. Behind him the Samnite awaits the decision of the public, whether he shall spare his vanquished foe, or put him to death.

The third couple represents a Thrax, or Thracian—so called from the fashion of his armour—and a Mirmillo, armed in the Gallic style. The latter, fifteen times a conqueror, now acknowledges a better than himself in

COMBAT BETWEEN A THRACIAN AND A MIRMILLO.

his opponent, who rejoices in his thirty-fifth victory. The letters M and θ over the Thracian's head stand for *Mors* and θανων, indicating that he was killed, according to the cruel law of the arena.*

In the next group there are four figures; two *secutores*, and two *retiarii*. Nepimus, one of the latter, five times victorious, has contended with a *secutor*—his name is lost, but Lord Lytton calls him Eumolpus—who has prevailed in six different combats. It is now his turn to

* Overbeck, "Pompeji," i. 176.

be defeated. Bleeding from the left arm, the leg, and the thigh, he has in vain implored the mercy of the spectators. The thumbs have been turned backwards. "And now, as the spear of the retiarius is not a weapon to inflict instant and certain death, there stalks into the arena a grim and fatal form, brandishing a short, sharp sword, and with features utterly concealed beneath its vizor. With slow and measured steps, this dismal headsman approaches the kneeling gladiator—lays the left hand on his humbled crest—draws the edge of the blade across his neck—turns round to the assembly, lest in the last moment remorse should come upon them; the dread signal continues the same; the blade glitters brightly in the air—falls—and the gladiator rolls upon the sand; his limbs quiver—are still—he is a corpse."

In the bas-relief the figure may be seen in the distance of the retiarius who is now to fight the victorious Nepimus, while the latter is shown (apparently) as pushing (or supporting?) his defeated and doomed rival.

This bas-relief terminates with an engagement between a light-armed gladiator and a Samnite. The latter implores the multitude to save him, but his appeal has not moved their iron hearts. The conqueror, looking towards the crowded amphitheatre, has seen the dread signal, and prepares to strike.

Following up the frieze, we find it continued between the pilasters of the door of the tomb. Here two combats are portrayed: in the first a Samnite has been vanquished by a Mirmillo, and the latter, in his bloodthirst, would fain become his comrade's executioner, even before the assembly to whom he has appealed pro-

COMBAT BETWEEN A MIRMILLO AND A SAMNITE.

nounces its decision. As the master of the show restrains his arm, we may infer that mercy has been shown the destined victim.*

COMBAT BETWEEN A LIGHT-ARMED GLADIATOR AND A SAMNITE.

In the other, a combat between a Samnite and a Mirmillo, the latter falls stabbed to death. The wounds,

* His name is given as Caius Ampliatus, who appears to have been a contractor for the supply of gladiators to the public shows.

the blood, and the inside of the bucklers are painted of a vivid red.

In some lower bas-reliefs we find various animated representations of the chase, and of combats between men and animals. Hares flee from the hound; a wounded stag, pursued by dogs, is about to become their prey; a wild boar falls a victim to the bold attack of a huge dog; and, in the centre of the composition, a *bestiarius* has slain a boar with a stroke of his lance. He wears a kind of short hunting-boot, and a light sleeveless tunic, bound about the hips, and called *indusia, sabucula*. His companion, similarly attired, has wounded a bull, which takes to flight, carrying in his chest the heavy spear with which he is transfixed. But he turns his head angrily towards his assailant, as if he would return to the assault; and the hunter stands amazed and somewhat alarmed; for he sees himself at the mercy of the animal whom he thought to have mortally stricken.

The reader will consider such subjects as these far from appropriate ornaments for the last resting-place of mortality.* Let him remember that they embellished a heathen's tomb. And for my part, I confess that I have seen even more repulsive sculptures on the sepulchres of many a Christian! It is strange how much of the old pagan spirit we still carry with us into the cemetery and the grave-yard; how we cling to the pagan emblems; how we picture Death itself with attributes derived not from the bright promises of Holy Writ, but from the

* These have been nearly all destroyed since 1830, but have fortunately been preserved by Mazois, Overbeck, and others, in engravings.

sombre meditations of the poets and moralists of antiquity.

Having thus detailed at some length, but not, I trust, to the reader's weariness, the arrangements and incidents of the Roman gladiatorial spectacles, a very few words

ARMING FOR THE COMBAT.

will suffice me for a description of the Amphitheatre at Pompeii.

The reader must not suppose it to have been an edifice worthy of comparison with the mighty Coliseum. It is smaller even than that of Capua, and more recent, though older than the great Roman structure. It is situated about 600 yards from the theatres, in the south-east angle of the city-walls, between the Gate of the Sarno and the Gate on the Nocera Road. Its form, as usual, is elliptical. The major axis, including the walls, is 430 feet; the minor axis, 335 feet; or 190 and 178 feet respectively, less than that of the Coliseum. The masonry is the rough work called *opus incertum*, with quoins of squared stone; the marble slabs with which it was formerly *veneered* were probably removed after the eruption. A few of the key-stones remain; on one a chariot and two horses (*biga*) is sculptured, on another a head.

At each end of the ellipse were entrances into the arena for the combatants, who, mounted or on foot, made their appearance to the ringing sound of the trumpet, and in stately procession completed a circuit of the building. The dead were dragged through the same portals into the spoliarium. They were also the principal approaches to the lower ranges of seats, occupied by the senators, magistrates, and equites, by means of corridors to the right and left, which ran round the arena. The ends of the passages were secured against the accidental inrush of wild beasts by metal gratings. The seats were elevated above the arena on a high *podium*, or parapet, which, when the amphitheatre was originally excavated, contained several inscriptions and paintings. The former recorded the names of duumvirs who had enlarged the building, or bestowed its site on the city, or presided over the games. The latter represented a battle between a bull and a bear, a stag pursued by a lioness, and a tigress contending with a wild boar. There were also fanciful designs of winged genii, minstrels, musicians, the palm-crowned gladiators, and candelabra; but on exposure to the atmosphere they rapidly vanished.

The interior contained four-and-twenty rows of seats, separated into different ranges, as already described; each range approached by a distinct entrance from two different galleries, of which the larger one had forty vomitories, communicating with the same number of *scalæ*—or flights of stairs dividing the seats into *cunei*. The arrangements for the egress and ingress of the assembly were perfect, and 10,000 spectators entered or dispersed with infinitely less confusion than the audience of a small London theatre. The arches of entrance were numbered, and the admission tickets—specimens of which are preserved in the Museum at Naples—bore corresponding numbers, so that every person proceeded to his proper seat without let or hindrance.

Outside the wall of the topmost gallery may be seen the perforated stones which received the poles or masts supporting the *velarium*, or awning. As this was of vast extent, to raise it to its place was a work of great labour and difficulty, and the means by which it was accomplished have been largely discussed by antiquarians. Of all the explanations I have met with, the following seems to my humble judgment the most probable :—

" The amphitheatre being oval, the velarium would of course be of the same form. We conjecture that a large oval ring of strong rope, about the size of the arena, was first formed, and divided into a certain number of equal parts by metal rings, corresponding in number and situation with the masts by which the awning was to be supported. To these rings long stout ropes would be attached, and rove through pulleys in the heads of the masts, the ends being brought down to the ground, and attached to windlasses. At a given signal this whole framework would begin to ascend by the slow action of the windlasses, and by a little dexterity the whole would be drawn equally tight, and the strain thrown equally on all the masts. The awning itself we imagine to have consisted of a number of pieces, either permanently attached to the framework of ropes, and drawn and un-

ANECDOTE OF COMMODUS.

drawn by an apparatus of smaller ropes and pulleys, or sent aloft at pleasure by similar means." *

It is recorded among the tyrannical caprices of Caligula, that on one occasion he ordered the velarium to be drawn back, and compelled the spectators in the Roman amphitheatre to sit in the full outpouring radiance of an Italian sun. The Emperor Commodus, who, vain of his gladiatorial skill, frequently descended into the arena,

CURRICLE OR CHARIOT BAR FOR TWO HORSES.
From a picture at Pompeii.

believed himself mocked by the crowd of servile Romans, when, on one occasion, they saluted him with divine honours, and ordered the sailors who were working the vela to fall upon them sword in hand. It was with difficulty that his favourites calmed his insane rage.

On the last day of Pompeii the amphitheatre was crowded with admiring spectators, at the very time that the sudden ruin fell upon the city. To this circumstance

* "Pompeii" (Library of Entertaining Knowledge), i. 295.

may be attributed the escape of so large a number of the inhabitants. When the hissing showers and hail of red-hot stones began, they immediately took to flight, and without attempting to regain their homes, poured through the gates of Nocera and the Sarno into the country beyond. Thus, in the midst of the revel and the festival, closed the history of a city whose whole career had been one of luxurious pleasure.

VI.

The Theatres.

"This player here,
But in a fiction, in a dream of passion,
Could force his soul to his own conceit,
That, from her working, all his visage wanned."
SHAKSPEARE.

THE quarter of the Theatres may be approached by two routes—by the Street of the Silversmiths on the eastern side, or by the street opening out at the south-eastern angle of the Forum. The space here excavated comprises two theatres, the greater and smaller; the barracks, or soldier's quarters; the Temple of Isis; the Temple of Hercules; and other minor edifices.

I shall devote this section to a description of the theatres, but to render it intelligible to the reader, a few prefatory remarks will be needed in reference to their general arrangement. It does not come within my province to explain the peculiarities of the Greek and Roman drama; but the reader will remember that the actors did not exhibit their skill, as with us, by mobility of feature and variety of expression, but solely depended on the excellence of their declamation and the grace or appropriateness of their gestures. The audience, therefore, so long as they could see and hear, did not require, as modern audiences do, to see and hear very distinctly. It was consequently possible for the ancients to erect huge theatres, in which a modern actor's voice would be lost, and from which no modern spectator could hope to watch the play of countenance that so eloquently illustrates the varying emotions. The Greek and Roman actors wore masks of brass, or some equally sonorous material, which gave the voice something of the power of a speaking-trumpet, and carried its sounds to an astonishing distance. It should also be remembered that the ancients did not require any rapid changes of scenery; and the reader will then understand why a Roman theatre differed very widely from an English one—why, in fact, the latter can only resemble the former in a few of its principal details.

The Roman theatre was a semicircular building, divided into two parts—the *cavea*, or auditory, and that appropriated to the business of the drama, which included, therefore, the orchestra and stage.

The *cavea* was bounded by two concentric circular arcs, one separating it from the orchestra and the other forming its external limit. It was composed of a succession of seats, as in an amphitheatre, rising tier above tier, so as to afford an uninterrupted view, and divided by numerous *scalæ* into compartments, or *cunei*, of equal dimensions. A vomitory corresponded to each scala. The lowest seats were appropriated to the magistrates and senators; fourteen rows behind them to the *equites;* and the remainder, or *popularia*, to the people. The foremost rows were called *cavea prima*, or *una;* the last, *cavea ultima,* or *summa;* the middle, *cavea media.*

The dramatic portions of the theatre were called the *scena, postscenium, proscenium, pulpitum,* and *orchestra.*

(*a.*) The *scena,* or scene, at the back of the proscenium, was richly adorned with gleaming statues, marble columns, pictures, and costly hangings, according to the character of the performance. Sometimes the decorations assumed a more romantic character, as Virgil hints in a well-known passage :—

> "High o'er the cove vast rocks extend,
> A beetling cliff at either end:
> Beneath their summit far and wide
> In sheltered silence sleeps the tide,
> While quivering forests crown the scene,
> A theatre of glancing green."

When the scene was suddenly changed by machinery, it was called *scena versatilis;* when simply drawn aside, *scena ductilis.*

The scenery was concealed by a curtain, which, contrary to our modern custom, was lowered when the play began, and raised at its conclusion ; this was effected by a machine called *exostra.*

(*b.*) The *postscenium,* the place behind the scenery, was the actors' dressing-room.

(*c.*) The *proscenium* corresponded to the modern stage. Here Medea declaimed her woes ; here Prometheus braved the wrath of Zeus ; here Ajax harangued the warrior Greeks. The deep passion of Æschylus, the tender pathos of Euripides, the grace of Sophocles, the keen flashing pregnant wit of Aristophanes, or the coarser humour of Plautus, and the *vis comica* of Terence, were here displayed before enchanted audiences. It was raised only five feet above the orchestra, with a door in the centre for the ingress and egress of kings and princes and mighty chieftains, and side-doors for meaner characters. The stage and postscenium were usually surrounded by elegant porticoes and blooming gardens. These buildings, being under cover, were more suitable for rehearsals than the open stage. A mosaic, discovered in a Pompeian house, exhibits the choragus, or stage-manager, in-

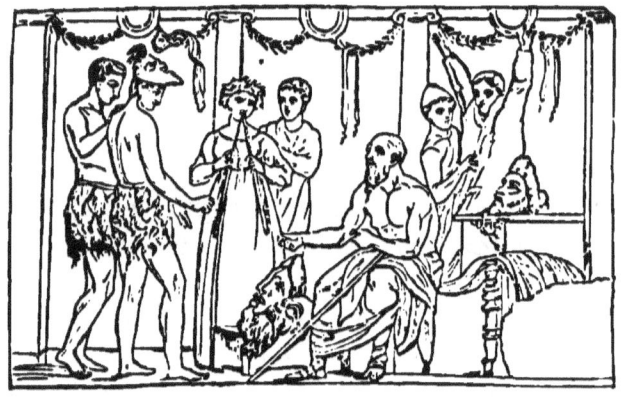

MOSAIC: REPRESENTING ACTORS INSTRUCTED BY THE CHORAGUS.

structing his actors in their parts. He is represented sitting on a chair in the choragium, or "green-room," surrounded by the performers—the "great tragedian," the "walking gentleman," the "leading lady," and other indispensable members of a well-regulated dramatic company. At his feet, on a stool, are the different masks which were used, and which were as various in expression as those in a modern pantomime; another is behind him, on a pedestal. One of the actors, assisted by a comrade, is attiring himself in a thick shaggy tunic; another has lifted his mask while receiving the instructions of the choragus. A female, crowned with a wreath, plays on the double flute, or tibia. Two figures wear nothing but goat-skins round their loins, as if the piece to be played were some Arcadian spectacle. The background shows the Ionic columns of the portico, decorated with festoons, and a gallery above, enriched with vases and statues. The whole is composed, like the modern Roman mosaics, of minute pieces of glass, and deserves commendation as a beautiful work of art.

(*d.*) The *pulpitum* was a broad shallow platform, which also formed a portion of what we should now-a-days call the stage. It was the part nearest the orchestra, where the actors stood when they spoke.

(*e.*) Lastly, the *orchestra* was a semicircular space between the pulpitum and the auditory, extending in front of the spectators, and somewhat below the lowest tier of seats. As its name indicates, it was the place, in the Greek theatre, where the chorus danced (ὀρχέομαι) and performed their evolutions, for which purpose it was covered with boards. But as the Roman drama had no chorus, the orchestra in a Roman theatre was appropriated for the seats of senators and other illustrious personages, such as foreign ambassadors, which were called "primus subselliorum ordo." *

I have already hinted that the rapid change of scenery which finds favour with modern audiences was unknown in Greek and Roman plays. Yet the piece was often

---

* Dr. Schmitz, in Smith's "Dictionary of Greek and Roman Antiquities," art. *Theatrum*.

"mounted"—to use a technical expression—with surprising magnificence, and the art of the painter was called in to supplement the art of the poet. No such mysterious illusions of perspective, or marvels of colour and design, or wonderful reproductions of actual landscape, or embodiments of fairy visions, as now astonish and delight us, ever astonished or delighted a Greek audience, but the spectacle set before them was often splendidly conceived. It has justly been remarked that the opening of the "Œdipus Tyrannus," with its crowd of citizens kneeling in awe-struck apprehension before the altar in the palace vestibule; or that grand scene in the "Prometheus," where the Titan, rock-bound in the desolate region of the Caucasus, is consoled by the airborne daughters of Ocean; or, I may add, the catastrophe of the "Medea," where the fate-driven murderess is swept away from human sight in her fiery car; and the grand contest in the "Ajax" for the armour of Achilles; may probably have vied, for picturesque effect, with the most successful achievements of modern machinists.

Those tragic flights, however, which so did take the imagination of the quick-witted Athenians, found but little favour with the Romans. The Eternal City could give birth to a Cicero and a Cæsar, but never rose to the dignity of an Æschylus or a Sophocles. Her tragic writers were but third-rate poets, and not a single Roman tragedy was ever composed on a Roman subject. There was more life, force, and originality in their comic dramas. In their mimes and burlesques, indeed, they rivalled the moderns. Their tumblers, their harlequins, their clowns, achieved feats of agility worthy of a Blondin or a Leotard.

THE FIRST THEATRES AT ROME. 133

They had their walkers upon stilts, their rope-dancers, their Merry-Andrews; and, as a crowning proof of their ingenuity in the "lower walks of the drama," let me record that they succeeded in teaching elephants to dance on the tight-rope, with riders and litters on their back!

MASKS, DWARF, AND MONKEY (FROM POMPEIAN FRESCO).

The earliest theatres at Rome were built of wood, and mere temporary buildings, removed when the occasion for them was over. Stage-players were first introduced in A.U.C. 391. The first exhibition of a dramatic performance after the Greek manner was given by Mummius, the destroyer of Corinth, about the year 610. The first permanent theatre was erected by Pompey in 699. Edifices of immense extent and unrivalled magnificence were also built by Scaurus and Curio, but these were of a temporary character. The former, according to Pliny, contained three hundred and threescore columns of marble, and could accommodate eighty thousand persons. The latter consisted of two theatres of timber, which were first used separately for dramatic entertainments, and then put together, face to face, as a circus for gladiatorial shows.

Pompey's theatre was injured by fire in the reign of Tiberius; restored by Caligula; again burned; and rebuilt by Claudius. A third time it was destroyed by fire, and re-erected by Titus.

The Theatre of Marcellus, built by Augustus, would contain thirty thousand persons. The splendour of its decorations is commemorated by the classic writers. A third theatre was raised by Cornelius Balbus, at the instance of Augustus.

The Pompeian theatres could not compare with those of Rome either in extent or magnificence, yet they would be considered worthy ornaments of any modern capital. The approach to them, when uninjured, must have combined both convenience and beauty.

Just at the point where the two streets from the Forum unite, stands a *propylæum* or *vestibule*, of eight Ionic columns, raised upon two steps, with a fountain in front of one of the columns, which poured its grateful waters through a sculptured mask of stone. This vestibule opens into an extensive Doric *colonnade*, retaining fragments of the iron bars anciently inserted between the pillars to confine the crowds within them. The colonnade is triangular in form; the eastern side measuring about 450 feet in length, the western nearly 300 feet. On these two sides extended a portico of ninety columns; the third side had no portico, but appears to have been lined with small offices. At different points were situated four entrances; three to the Great Theatre, and one to the barracks for the troops.

Within the ample area or piazza thus formed—sometimes called the *Triangular Forum*—moulder the ruins of a sacred edifice, called, from its style of architecture, the Greek Temple, otherwise the *Temple of Hercules*. It is the most ancient building yet discovered in the "City of the Dead," and from its elevated position must have formed a conspicuous landmark to all mariners navigating the Parthenopean waters. Some authorities date the erection about eight hundred years before Christ. If this be true, it must have been built by some of the earliest colonists, who, migrating from Cumæ, or the shores of Hellas, planted themselves at the vine-clad base of Vesuvius. At all events, it possesses in itself—in its massive Doric columns, its deep and boldly projecting abaci, and the general details of its construction— abundant evidence of its remote antiquity.

The whole building seems to have stood upon a podium or basement, raised five steps above the level of the ground. It was 120 feet in length, and 70 feet in breadth. Its cella, divided into several compartments, was paved with mosaics, the masonry covered with stucco. A curious enclosure in front of the steps is supposed to have been a pen to contain victims—two altars standing by its side. A few paces distant are the remains of a small circular temple of eight Doric columns of tufa, covering a *purteal* or well, protected by a circular perforated altar. Either the water required for the sacrifices was obtained from hence, or it was a sacred spot—a *bidental*, or *locus fulminatus*—where a thunderbolt had fallen. Such a place was always regarded by the Romans with peculiar sanctity. It was not allowable to touch, to tread on, or to look at it. Whoever profaned it would be punished by the gods with madness. To violate its hallowed precincts was a foul sacrilege.*

* Horace, "Ars Poetica" (Epist. ad Pison.), 471.

It has been conjectured that this most ancient and venerable pile, where the monotonous chant of the priests was heard, and the bleeding sacrifices smoked some two thousand six hundred and sixty years ago, was erected on the site of a pottery of still older date, whose *débris* have been discovered beneath its base. The spot is elevated several hundred feet above the level of the plain which it overlooks, on what was in fact the crest, the apex of the isolated eminence which bore the houses, and temples, and theatres of Pompeii. An *exedra*, or semi-circular seat, at the south-west angle of the building, is so placed as to command every detail in a most gorgeous and extensive panorama. I wish that I possessed the pen of a Ruskin to describe its wealth of beauty, its plenitude of inspiration. Little idea could the reader form of all that renders it attractive, from any cold, dull inventory-like enumeration of sapphire skies, and misty uplands, and azure seas. But let him remember that the view I speak of includes the chestnut-shaded hill of Castellamare—the olive-groves and rocky heights of Vico—the vineyards, the mulberry-trees, the pomegranates, the richly wooded valleys, and sea-washed cliffs of Tasso's Sorrento—the smiling isle of Capri, where Tiberius revelled in the luxury of vice—and the broad unruffled azure of that beautiful bay which he who has once seen never forgets, the full outline of those Parthenopéan shores, which song and fable have rendered famous, and art and nature inexpressibly lovely;—let him remember this, I say, and he will own that the scene might task the pencil of a Claude or a Turner, and inspire the most melodious song of a Shelley or a Keats, the former to realize its inner sense of beauty, the latter to embody its wonderful richness of form and colour!

The city wall appears to have bounded the portico on the southern side, while parallel to the eastern runs a long low wall, terminated at the one end by the altars and bidental already mentioned, and at the other by a pedestal inscribed :—*

M . CLAUDIO . M . F . MARCELLO . PATRONO.

I have said that there were three—or rather four— entrances from the eastern side of the piazza to different parts of

THE GREAT THEATRE.

The two first, as you enter, open upon a large circular corridor surrounding the entire *cavea*. The third leads into an area behind the scene, from which a communication is made with the orchestra, and the *primus subselliorum ordo*—or what we English designate "orchestra-stalls;" the fourth led down a long flight of steps, at the bottom of which you turn to the right for the so-called Soldiers' Barracks, to the left for the area already mentioned. The corridor is vaulted: it has two other entrances, one by a large passage from the east, and another from a smaller passage on the north. Six inner doors, or *vomitoria*, opened on an equal number of staircases leading to the first *præcinctio*.†

The theatre is placed on the southern slope of the hill, the corridor being the highest part, so that the audience, upon entering, descended immediately to their

* Overbeck, " Pompeji," *in loco*.
† " Pompeii" (Library of Entertaining Knowledge), i. 260, 261.

seats. By the side of the first entrance is a staircase leading up to the gallery where the women sat, for in the ancient theatres they were separated from the men. What a display of gems and embroidered robes, of towering head-dresses and flashing eyes, must that gallery have presented; a mass of the dark-haired, dark-eyed women of the South congregated in one restricted space —enough, methinks, to have shaken the confidence of the most self-possessed of actors ! The seats here were divided into compartments, like our boxes; each seat being about fifteen inches high, and two feet four inches wide. What think you was the space allotted to each Pompeian dame? Exactly one foot three inches and a half! I should like to see an English lady, *en grande tenue*, accommodating herself within such circumscribed limits! But, owing to this arrangement, space was obtained for seating—English ladies would say *crowding* —about five thousand persons. *

The middle classes usually sat upon cushions, which they brought with them; patricians on chairs of state, carried to the theatre by their slaves. Flanking the orchestra, but raised considerably above it, may be observed two divisions whose appropriation is somewhat uncertain. One, however, we may suppose to have been reserved for the Roman proconsul, or the duumvirs and their suite; the other for the vestal virgins, or for the giver of the entertainments. This is the more probable, says an authority of great credit, because in the smaller theatre, where these boxes, if we may call them so, are also found, they have a communication with the stage.

* For a good description of a Roman theatre, see Bekker's "Gallus."

How splendid an appearance must this structure have presented in its palmy days! It must have gleamed and glittered in the sunshine like a fairy pile; the walls cased with marble, the benches of marble, the orchestra of marble, the scena, with its decorations—all of marble ; but of this magnificence, and its statues, and its scenic embellishments, scarce a vestige remains. There can be no doubt that it escaped the more destructive effects of the eruption, owing to its elevated position and the great height of its outer work, and that the citizens afterwards returned and removed its more precious spoils.

From an inscription formerly found in it, on the first step of the orchestra, with a central space for a statue, it appears that the theatre, as well as a crypt, and the tribunal, was erected by Marcus Holconius Rufus, Duumvir, Military Tribune, and Patron of the Colony, and that the decurions reared the statue in grateful acknowledgment of his services.*

Let us now suppose we are viewing the interior from one of the entrances leading to the orchestra. On the right hand is the scena. From what remains it can be seen that the three principal doors were deeply recessed; those at the sides rectangular, the central one circular. In front of the latter stood two columns. Behind it is the postscenium. From the eastern side of the stage a covered portico led into the orchestra of the small theatre, and was intended, perhaps, as a communication between the privileged seats of either house, for the accommodation of those entitled to make use of them.

* Overbeck, " Pompeji," i. 145.

A VIEW OF THE INTERIOR.

In the wall supporting the front of the stage are seven recesses, similar to those discovered in the theatre at Herculaneum. There can be little doubt that these were occupied by the musicians.

In front is the entrance to the orchestra. Above may be seen the six rows of steps which encircled it; then the *cavea*, despoiled of its marble, but still exhibiting the lines of benches—summa cavea, media cavea, and infima cavea—the stairs, or *scalæ*, dividing them into *cunei*—and the *vomitoria*, or doors of entrance. Higher still is the women's gallery; and above that the external wall, which, as it was never entirely buried, should surely have pointed out to any observant traveller the exact situation of the lost Pompeii.

COMIC SCENE (FROM A PAINTING AT POMPEII).

The same general plan and disposition of parts were observed in

THE SMALL THEATRE, OR ODEUM.

In form, however, it is different; it approaches nearer to a rectangle, the semicircle being cut off by straight walls from each end of the stage. A still more noticeable difference is, that it was *permanently roofed*, as appears from the following inscription :—

> C . QVINCTIVS . C . F . VALG.
> M . PORCIVS . M . F.
> DVO . VIR . DEC . DECR.
> THEATRVM . TECTVM.
> FAC . LOCAR . EIDEMQ . PROB.
>
> [Caius Quinctius Valgus, son of Caius, and Marcus Porcius, son of Marcus, Duumvirs, by a decree of the Decurions, let out the covered theatre to be erected by contract, and the same approved it.]

Either because built by contract, or because of greater antiquity, it is inferior to the other theatre in construction and decoration. It is supposed to have been erected shortly after the end of the Social War, and may have been used for dramatic entertainments when the state of the weather prevented open-air performances.

The material employed is tufa (from Nocera), except that the scalæ are constructed of hard Vesuvian lava, well suited to resist the constant action of ascending and descending feet. The scena, the front wall of the proscenium, and the pavement of the orchestra, were entirely marble; marble of various colours—African breccia, purple, and giallo antico. A band of marble, in white and gray stripes, traverses it from end to end of the seats, with inlaid letters of bronze, eight and a half inches long, and level with the surface, forming the following inscription :—

> M . OCVLATIVS . M . F . VERVS . DVIR . PRO . LVDIS.
>
> [Marcus Oculatius Verus, son of Marcus, Duumvir for the Games.]

The pavement was probably laid down at the expense of this munificent Pompeian.

Within the orchestra itself were four tiers of benches for the *bisellia*, or chairs of state, in which the magistrates and great men of the city sat. The bisellium was usually made of bronze, richly ornamented with silver, and supported on four upright legs. Two inscriptions in the Street of Tombs lead us to infer that the right of using it was a highly prized distinction, and only granted

FRESCO—A LANDSCAPE. (FOUND AT POMPEII.)

as a mark of honour to distinguished persons by the magistrates and people in provincial towns. Though large enough to contain two persons, only one occupied it; hence its name. The *sella curulis*, or curule chair of state, was confined to Roman magistrates, or to the proconsuls and prætors of the provinces.

The seats of the audience were separated by a passage from the tiers of benches which held the bisellia. This passage was bounded on the side of the stage by a high parapet, ornamented with winged griffins' legs; on the side of the cavea, by a wall, terminating in two kneeling Herculean figures, which are supposed to have sustained bronze candelabra.

The cavea contained seventeen rows of seats, and the whole theatre could probably accommodate fifteen hundred persons.

Adjoining the small theatre stands a large rectangular enclosure, which has been variously called *Forum Nundinarium*, or the provision market; and

THE SOLDIERS' BARRACKS.

It measures 183 feet in length by 158 in width, and is surrounded by a Doric colonnade, with twenty-two columns on the longer, and seventeen on the shorter sides. These columns are covered with stucco; one-third (the lower) is plain and painted red; the upper portion fluted, and coloured alternately red and yellow.

Under the colonnade are numerous small tenements, which, it is conjectured, were occupied by butchers, and vendors of vegetables, meats, and liquors. One appears to have been the soldiers' mess-room; another the guard-room; a third, the prison; in a fourth, utensils for the manufacture of soap, and in a fifth, an oil-mill, have been discovered. There are also stables, a kitchen with all the necessary adjuncts, and stables for the horses.

Above was a second story, approached by three narrow flights of steps, as well as by a staircase of better construction, probably leading to the officers' chambers.

A wooden gallery running all round it afforded a means of communication from one room to another.

It has been matter of dispute whether this building was appropriated as a barrack for the Roman garrison, or as a school for gladiators. The balance of evidence seems to me strongly in favour of the former hypothesis. Over the whole spreads, if I may use the expression, a strong flavour of military life. Among the articles discovered here, for instance, were bronze and iron helmets, shields, greaves for the legs, lances, swords, leather belts, strigils, sword-belts of bronze richly ornamented, officers' helmets finely inlaid or covered with admirable bas-reliefs, ivory-handled swords, and numerous matters of feminine attire belonging, we may conjecture, to members of the officers' families. Among the latter were gilt pins for the hair, chests of cloth of gold and delicate white linen, ear-rings, jewelled bracelets, finger-rings of gold, and costly necklaces—all indicative of luxurious and careful toilets. In the guard-room four skeletons were found, with their legs fixed in strong iron stocks. An upper chamber contained eighteen skeletons of men, women, and children, one of an infant, and several of dogs—all surprised at the same moment by an inevitable death. Under the stairs reclined a human skeleton holding a cup of silver. Was he endeavouring to escape with it? Or had he descended in quest of a draught of wine? Inside one of the entrance gates thirty-four skeletons lay in dread companionship—those of the guard, doubtless, who had been summoned hastily at the outbreak of the catastrophe, and overtaken by the Invisible before they could dispose themselves in military array. The total number of skeletons discovered among these ruins was sixty-three.

Behind the two theatres, and at the corner of the street of Stabiæ, stands the so-called

TEMPLE OF ÆSCULAPIUS,

excavated in 1766—so called by Winckelmann, but perhaps more generally known as the Theatre of Jupiter and Juno. It is a small but well-proportioned building, raised on a low basement of nine steps, and comprising a small cella, with a tetrastyle pseudo-dystoral portico— that is, with an external range of columns surrounding the entire building. In the open court stands a large altar, closely resembling the monument in the Vatican known as the Tomb of the Scipios—the frieze being composed of triglyphs with volutes at the corners. The cella contained, when discovered, three terra-cotta statues of Æsculapius, Hygeia, and Priapus.*

Between the theatres and the temple we observe the

HOUSE OF THE SCULPTOR,

remarkable only for its contents (now in the Neapolitan Museum), which illustrated the ancient practice of the "plastic art." Some statues were found here, half finished; others, just mere blocks of marble, whose future proportions had scarcely been outlined by the sculptor's hand. Here, too, compasses, calipers, proportional compasses, rules and weights for drawing perpendicular lines and levelling, thirty-two mallets, three

* Overbeck, "Pompeji."

or four levers, numerous chisels, and several saws, attested the nature of the owner's occupation. In the midst of his work the doom had fallen on the city, and he was suddenly called away from all his bright dreams of the ideal, all his vivid conceptions of the beautiful, all his essays to give a visible embodiment to those dreams and those conceptions—to give a "local habitation" to those "airy nothings" of the fervid brain. Did he ever resume the task, I wonder? Or was he, too, among the victims of the volcanic eruption?

Returning westward, along the northern side of the piazza, we arrive at a remarkable structure, the Temple of Isis, or

THE ISEON.

It was but of recent erection at the date of the destruction of Pompeii, an older building having been demolished in the earthquake of the year 63. It stood on a slightly elevated basement in the centre of an open court, surrounded by a Corinthian portico of painted columns, each column about one foot nine inches in diameter. To the two nearest the entrance two lustred marble basins were formerly attached, and a wooden box, reduced to charcoal, probably intended as a receptacle for the contributions of worshippers. Over the entrance was the following inscription :—

N. POPIDIVS . N. F. CELSINVS.
ÆDEM . ISIDIS . TERRÆ . MOTV . CONLAPSAM
A . FVNDAMENTIS . P. SVA . RESTITVIT.
HVNC . DECVRIONES . OB . LIBERALITATEM .
CVM. ESSET. ANNORVM. SEXS. ORDINI . SVO.
GRATIS . ADLEGERVNT.

[Numerinus Popidius Celsinus, son of Numerinus, restored from the foundation, at his own expense, the Ædes of Isis, overthrown by an earthquake. The Decurions, on account of his liberality, elected him, when sixty years of age, to be one of their order without paying fees.]

The reader will observe that this building was an Ædes, and not a Templum; that is, it had never been consecrated by the pontiff and augurs, for the worship of Isis had been forbidden by a decree of the Roman Senate in B.C. 57. It was nevertheless very popular in Italy, where it had been introduced in the time of Sulla.* The Roman ladies especially loved to patronize its ceremonies, which combined licentiousness with mystery in a peculiarly piquant manner. The oracles of the goddess at Pompeii, says Lord Lytton, were remarkable, not more for the mysterious language in which they were clothed, than for the credit which was attached to their mandates and predictions. "If they were not dictated by a divinity, they were framed at least by a profound knowledge of mankind; they applied themselves exactly to the circumstances of individuals, and made a notable contrast to the vague and loose generalities of their rival temples."

Altars were erected on each side of the portico; a Corinthian portico of six columns, flanked by two wings, with niches for the reception of statues. The walls of the altar, elevated on seven steps of Parian marble, were also adorned with statues, and with the pomegranate symbol consecrated to Isis. An oblong pedestal occupied the interior building, on which stood two images,— one of the great Egyptian goddess; the other of the

* Dr. Smith's "Dictionary of Greek and Roman Biography," art. *Isis*.

silent Orus—the Greek Harpocrates—with finger on his lips as if to enjoin on the worshippers a reverent silence regarding the mysteries displayed before them. Isis was attired in purple drapery, holding a bronze sistrum—a mystical instrument of music peculiar to her worship*— and a key, indicative of her power to unlock the secrets of the universe, or to open the flood-gates of the Nile. The building contained many other deities to grace the court of the Egyptian goddess; her kinsman Bacchus or Dionysius,—the Cyprian Venus, a Greek disguise for herself, rising from her bath,—the dog-headed Anubis,— the ox Apis, and various Egyptian idols of uncouth form. The walls were covered with allegorical pictures, fantastically painted, but of great interest from their reference to Isiac mysteries. The pedestal was hollow, with two low apertures at the end near the secret stairs, so that the priests, ascending, could enter it unperceived, and astonish the deluded crowd by delivering the responses as if from the very statue of the goddess. These priests were known by the general name of *Isiaca*. According to Herodotus, they were forbidden to eat the flesh of swine or sheep. They shaved their heads, and wore shoes of papyrus, and garments of linen, because Isis first taught the use of linen, and was therefore called *Linigera*, or the "linen-bearing." In their temples they burned gums in the morning, myrrh at noon, and kyphy

---

* It consisted of a semicircular frame, crossed by four bars, which gave forth, when shaken, a shrill loud sound. Plutarch says, the shaking of the bars within the circular apsis symbolized the agitation of the four elements within the compass of the world, by which all things are continually destroyed and reproduced. The cat sculptured upon it represented the moon.—Dr. Smith, "Dictionary of Antiquities," art. *Sistrum*, p. 1046.

ISIAC MYSTERIES. 149

—an unknown mixture of sixteen substances—in the evening. Notwithstanding their vows of chastity, they were a dissolute and vicious fraternity, and contributed largely to that moral corruption which undermined the stability of the Roman empire. The forms and ceremonies introduced by them into the Italian cities were but burlesques of the rules of the old Egyptian worship. The profound mysteries of the Nile, it has been well observed, were degraded by a hundred meretricious and frivolous admixtures from the creeds of Cephissus and of Tiber.

In the south-east corner of the temple enclosure stands an *ædiculum*, or chapel—a small building ornamented with pilasters, with an arched opening in the centre, and over the arch a representation of figures in the act of adoration; a vase is placed between them. The ædiculum covered the sacred well, used for the purification of the worshippers, and is embellished with elegant though capricious arabesques in green, and yellow, and red. Near it is an altar, on which were discovered the charred remains of the sacrifice; and the wall adjoining is still discoloured with the smoke of the sacrificial fire. Other altars or pedestals remain within the enclosure; and on the two flanking the steps which ascend to the temple were found two Isiac tables of basalt, covered with hieroglyphics, now in the Museum at Naples.*

In the south side, opposite the entrance from the street, were the chambers for the priests, and a kitchen in which they cooked their food. A skeleton lay in the

* Pompeii ("Library of Entertaining Knowledge"), i. 279.

outer room, conjectured to be that of a priest, who, having found his escape at the door blocked up by the fast falling ashes, had striven to cut his way through the walls with an axe; through two, indeed, he had hewn a passage, but before he could pass the third, was stifled by the deadly vapour. The axe was found lying by his remains. Behind the temple is a large chamber, forty-two feet by twenty-five, in which another skeleton was discovered. He seems, like his comrade, to have been at dinner when the supreme hour of Pompeii came. In the sacred precincts lay many other skeletons, probably those of the Isiaci, who, reposing an empty confidence in the power of their deity, or stricken by panic fear, had cowered around the desolate altars, until overtaken by the deadly torrent of ashes. Faithful to their goddess to the last, they perished in the very blindness of their superstitious devotion.*

From the area, once sacred to the worship of the Egyptian divinity, we pass onward to

THE TRIBUNAL,

formerly called the *Curia Isiaca*, and the "School," an oblong open court, 79 feet long by 57 feet wide, surrounded

---

* Isis, fabled to be the wife of Osiris, is said, from the Coptic word *Isi*, to mean "abundance." Some identify her with Pallas, others with Ceres; but she is mostly represented as the goddess of the Moon, the Horn-bearing (κεραόφορος), from the lunar changes; also, the Dark-robed (μελανότολος), because she shines through the night. Under the name "Isis," the word Wisdom was occasionally understood; and in her temple was this inscription :—" I am the All that was, that is, that shall be; no mortal can lift my veil." Wonderful medicinal powers were ascribed to her; and many diseases, it was supposed, originated in her wrath. She was believed to be the inventor of several medicines—even of the healing art itself; and, therefore, the Romans called an universal medicine, *Isis*.—Ennemoser, "History of Magic," i. 244, 245.

MYTHOLOGICAL FRESCOES.

on three sides by a portico of the Doric order, with two chambers at one end, supposed to be the crypt, and an elevated *pulpitum* for the judge at the side. Its uses cannot be accurately determined, but it seems to have been the tribunal alluded to in an inscription found in the Greater Temple :—

M. M. HOLCONI . RVFVS FI . CELER
CRYPTAM . TRIBVNAL . THEATRVM. S. P.
AD . DECVS. COLONIÆ.

[Marcus Holconius Rufus, son of Marcus, built the crypt, tribunal, and theatre, for the honour of the city (*colonia*).]

With a word of reference to a small but elegant house, provided with a peristyle and impluvium, which was situated nearly opposite the Iseon, in the street of Stabiæ, and in one of whose rooms may be seen a rude but vigorous picture of Hercules disguised among the daughters of Omphale, — as well as a cleverly designed group of Venus and Adonis,— we take our leave of the so-called Triangular Forum, and all its memorials of a strange but interesting antiquity.

MYTHOLOGICAL FRESCOES (FOUND AT POMPEII).

VII.

The Thermæ, or Baths.

" The garlands, the rose-odours, and the flowers."
BYRON.

*" All through the lorn
Vacuity, winds come and go, but stir
Only the flowers of yesterday."*
SYDNEY DOBELL.

AMONG the public edifices of Rome, scarcely any were more deserving of admiration, on account either of their magnitude, their architectural splendour, or their internal decorations, than the Thermæ, or Public Baths. These colossal structures were all arranged on a common plan : they were surrounded by a colonnade of shapely pillars, and stood among well-ordered walks and extensive gardens, which were decorated with leafy groves, with statues, and with sparkling fountains. The main building contained not only ample accommodation for bathing and swimming, but salons for the conversation of lounging patricians, halls suitable for gymnastic exercises, and rotundas where philosophers might argue and poets declaim. These chambers were of noble construction, were paved and lined with marble, glittered with bust and statue and painting, and were provided with libraries for the recreation of the studious.

The Thermæ were, in fact, for Rome what the clubs are for aristocratic London, except that the public were admitted to them gratuitously, and that they were available for the lower classes as freely as for the wealthiest patricians.

It is not the province of the present writer to describe the Roman Baths; yet it seems desirable to afford the reader some idea of their arrangement, as they were the models on which those of Pompeii were fashioned. Eustace, an author of eloquence and judgment, thus describes the present condition of the *Thermæ* of Caracalla, among whose ruins, led me add, the poet Shelley wrote his drama of "Prometheus Unbound." They occupy part of the declivity of the Aventine hill, and a considerable portion of the low ground between it, Mons Cœliolus, and Mons Cœlius. "The length of the Thermæ," he says, "was 1840 feet, its breadth 1476. At each end were two temples,—one to Apollo and another to Æsculapius, as the tutelary deities (*genii tutelares*) of a place sacred to the improvement of the mind and the cure of the body. The two other temples were dedicated to the two protecting divinities of the Antonine family, Hercules and Bacchus.

"In the principal building were, in the first place, a grand circular vestibule, with four halls on each side for cold, tepid, warm, and steam baths; in the centre was an immense square for exercise, when the weather was unfavourable to it in the open air; beyond it a great hall, where 1600 marble seats were placed for the convenience of the bathers; at each end of this hall were libraries. This building terminated on both sides in a court surrounded with porticoes, with an Odeum for music; and in the middle a spacious basin for swimming. Round this edifice were walks shaded by rows of trees, particularly the plane; and in its front extended a gymnasium for running, wrestling, &c., in fine weather. The whole was bounded by a vast portico opening into exedræ, or spacious halls, where the poets declaimed and philosophers gave lectures to their auditors.

"This immense fabric was adorned within and without with pillars, stucco-work, paintings, and statues. The stucco and paintings, though faintly indeed, are yet in many places perceptible. Pillars have been dug up, and some still remain amidst the ruins; while the Farnesian Bull and the famous Hercules, found in one of these halls, announce the multiplicity and beauty of the statues which once adorned the Thermæ of Caracalla. The flues and reservoirs of water still remain. The height of the pile was proportioned to its extent, and still appears very considerable, even though the ground be raised at least twelve feet above its ancient level. It is now changed into vineyards and gardens, its high massive walls form separations, and its tiny ruins, spread over the surface, burn the soil and check its natural fertility."*

Pompeii, I need hardly say, could boast of no such imperial pile as this; yet were its Thermæ very compactly and handsomely arranged, and decorated with much artistic excellence. I shall now attempt a description of them, and conclude my description with a sketch of the processes of ablution carried on within their walls.

The Thermæ, or Public Baths, discovered in 1814, is

* Eustace, "A Classical Tour through Italy," i. 226, *sqq.*

a considerable establishment, having a frontage towards three streets, and a principal entrance from the Street of Fortune. All or most of the rooms opening into the street, on each side this entrance, seem to have been vaulted, and so were made to contribute to the support of the arches thrown over the larger chambers in the interior.

This entry, or passage, opened into a court about 60 feet long, bounded on two sides by a Doric portico (*ambulacrum*), and on the third by a crypt. The seats, which may be seen arranged round the walls, accommodated the slaves while waiting for their masters. In this court were found a sword with a leather sheath, which, perhaps, belonged to the balneator, or keeper of the baths, and the box for the quadrans, or piece of money, which was paid by each visitor. The quadrans was the fourth part of the assis, and the fourteenth of the denarius, a sum so small that the cost of heating of the baths could not have been defrayed without a crowd of bathers.*
We must, however, remember that many Romans bathed seven times in a day. Horace playfully alludes to the trifling sum at which they thus made themselves supremely happy:—

"Dum tu quadrante lavatum
Rex ibis."

While you can bathe for a quadrans, he says, you are as happy as a king!—In the great Thermæ of imperial Rome no charge at all was made for admission.

In the Doric portico, persons waited for admission to the Thermæ, which could not conveniently accommodate

* Sir W. Gell, "Pompeiana," i. 91.

more than thirty bathers at a time. Here, therefore, notices might suitably be exposed of public games, exhibitions, and festivals. And here, on the south wall, still may be read the following inscription, carrying back the mind at one sudden bound over the crowded space of eighteen hundred years:—

                          MAIO
DEDICATI (ᴘᴏʟʏ) NE   PRINCIPI COLONIÆ
                          FELICITER
. . . . RVM . MVNERIS . CN. ALLEI NIGIDI MAI.
. . . . VENATIO . ATHLETAE . SPARSIONES . VELA. ERUNT.

[At the dedication of the Baths, at the expense of Cnæus Alleius Nigidius Maius, there will be a venatio, athletic contests, sprinkling of perfumes, and awnings. Prosperity to Maius, chief of the colony.]*

From this inscription, it appears that the dedication or inauguration of the Baths was celebrated by public games at the cost of a liberal or popularity-hunting citizen, named Maius, who had probably been selected by the magistracy for this expressive honour. Evidently he celebrated the event with great pomp. There were combats between wild beasts, or between wild beasts and men, gymnastic exercises, wrestling, leaping, throwing, and the like; while, to increase the comfort of the spectators, awnings would be spread as a protection from the burning sun, and the warm air tempered by showers of perfumed water. †

From the court we pass, by a small corridor, into the

---

* The word *poly*, in the centre of the letter O, signifies "many," in Latin as well as in Greek.

† According to Seneca, the perfumes were dispersed abroad by being mixed with boiling water, and then placed in the centre of the amphitheatre, so that rising with the vapour, they floated throughout the building.

apodyterium, or undressing-room, which is also accessible by another corridor from a street now called the Street of the Arch. Here were found above five hundred lamps of terra-cotta, and upwards of a thousand were collected in the whole circuit of the baths. Some were embellished with figures of the Graces, and others with the image of Harpocrates, but some were very artistically wrought. The ceiling of this passage is decorated with stars.

The apodyterium (also called the spoliatorium or apodyterium) derives its name from the Ἀποδυτήμα of the Greeks. It was here the bathers undressed; and you still observe the holes in the walls in which were inserted the pegs for hanging up their togas, their tunics, or their pallia. Three seats made of lava were also provided for their accommodation.

The chamber itself, which was always moderately warmed, is spacious, and stuccoed from the cornice to the ground, the stucco being highly finished and coloured yellow. The cornice, of large dimensions, has "something of an Egyptian character;" the carved frieze below it is sprawled all over with dolphins, griffins, lyres, and vases, on a red ground. The floor is handsomely paved with white marble wrought in mosaic; the ceiling consisted of white panels within vermilion-coloured borders. A little apartment at the north end was either a latrina, or, if the light were sufficient, a tonstrina for shaving; or more probably it was a closet where the unguents, strigils, and towels required by the bather were generally kept.

There are six doors. One leading to the præpurnium;

another into the above-mentioned chamber; the third, by a narrow corridor, to the Street of the Arch; the fourth, to the tepidarium; the fifth, to the frigidarium; and the sixth, along a corridor, to the vestibule or portico of the Thermæ.

In the centre of the end wall of the room, a small recess, once covered with a piece of glass, contained a lamp. In the archivolt, or vaulted roof, immediately above this recess, was placed a window, 2 feet 8 inches high, and 3 feet 8 inches broad, closed by a single large pane of cast glass, two-fifths of an inch thick, fixed into the wall, and ground on one side, so that persons on the roof might be prevented from curiously prying into the apodyterium. No error has been more general, and yet more absurdly unfounded, than that the use of glass was very limited among the ancients. The fact is, that they had attained to considerable excellence in its manufacture. They imitated every known marble and every precious stone, and employed these admirable imitations in cups and vases of every size and shape. A few years later than the destruction of Pompeii we read of the *calices alla-sontes*, or glass goblets, which shone with shifting prismatic colours. Whole chambers even were lined with this radiant material. In the time of Seneca the chambers in the Thermæ had their walls covered with glass and Thasian marble, the water issued from tubes of silver, and the principal decorations were mirrors of various sizes.

That the ancients were well acquainted with the art of glass-blowing in all its branches, is evident from the vast collection of bottles, glasses, and other utensils discovered among the ruins of Pompeii.

To return to the apodyterium. In the window-lighted compartment already spoken of, a large bas-relief in stucco was found, whose subject seems to have been the overthrow of the Titans by Jove (or Saturn?), whose colossal head figures conspicuously in the centre.*

Passing into the *frigidarium*,† or cold bath, we see before us a circular chamber, lined with stucco, which appears to have been painted originally in yellow and green. The roof, in the form of a truncated cone, was coloured blue. It had an opening, or window, near the top, from which it was lighted.

In each angle of the room, which may be strictly described as a circle enclosed by a square, an alcove is placed, called by the ancients *schola*, a word derived from the Hebrew, and signifying repose. Each is 5 feet 2 inches wide, by 2 feet $\frac{1}{2}$ inch deep; the wall painted blue, the conca or cove red, and the arch encircled with a relieved border in stucco. In these niches were seats for the convenience of the bathers.

About eight feet from the floor, a cornice encircles the entire chamber, nearly eighteen inches high, coloured red, and adorned in stucco with the representation of a chariot-race of Cupids,—with Cupids on horseback and on foot guiding and encouraging the competitors; the whole distinguished by a remarkable air of truth and

---

* Such is the description given by Sir W. Gell. Another authority gives a curiously different version :—" A large mask is moulded in stucco, with curling hair and a most venerable floating beard. Water is sculptured flowing from the locks of hair, and on each side two Tritons, with vases on their shoulders, are fighting. There are also dolphins, who encircle with their tails the figures of children struggling to disengage themselves."—*Pompeii*, vol. i. p. 157.

† Called the Natatio, by Sir W. Gell.—" Pompeiana," vol. i. p. 100.

lifelike spirit. The plinth, or base of the wall, is of marble; so is the pavement of the floor, and the seat or step which surrounds the central basin.

THE FRIGIDARIUM.

The basin in the centre of the room (*alveus*) measures 12 feet 10 inches in diameter, 2 feet 9 inches in depth, and is entirely lined with white marble. The bather descended into it by two marble steps, and at the bottom was a species of cushion (*pulvinus*), also of marble, on which, if so disposed, he might rest himself. The water ran into this bath in a large stream, through a spout or lip of bronze four inches wide, placed in the wall at the height of 3 feet 7 inches from the edge of the basin. There was an outlet for the superfluous water; and, in all, a depth of about three feet for the bather. It was, therefore, what we should call a cold bath, and by no means a swimming bath according to our English notions. What athletic Britain, indeed, would care for a plunge into an artificial pond, about 31 feet in circumference, and only three feet in depth? Half-a-dozen strokes would complete its circuit! We are told, however, that the *natatorium* of the Baths of Diocletian, at Rome, was 200 feet long, and about half that width; the Aqua Martia supplying copious streams of water, which welled forth in quaint artificial grottoes. The Pompeian piscina can make no pretensions to vie with such imperial magnificence, but not the less it is elegantly and skilfully designed.

Through folding doors the bather, when his frame had been hardened by the cold-water baths, passed into the *Tepidarium*, or warm chamber, where a soft and genial temperature insensibly prepared him for the intense heat of the vapour and hot baths, or, *vice versa*, mitigated the transition from those to the external air.* It was warmed by a twofold agency: first, by means of a suspended pavement heated by the distant fires of the stove of the *calidarium*; secondly, by means of a brazier (*foculare*) 7 feet long and 2 feet 6 inches broad, made entirely of

* Dr. Smith's "Dictionary of Greek and Roman Antiquities," art. *Balneæ*.

bronze, with the exception of an iron casing. The two hind legs are plain, the two front are winged sphinxes, terminating in lions' paws. The bottom consists of brass bars. Bricks were laid on these, and on the bricks lumps of pumice-stone, while the fire was made with charcoal.* The rim is ornamented by thirteen battle-mented summits, a lotus at the angles, and the figure of a cow beneath.

For the accommodation of the bathers three seats of bronze were provided, all of the same form and design. They were 1 foot 4 inches high, 1 foot wide, and about 6 feet long; and inscribed with the name of the donor, thus :—

M. NIGIDIVS . VACCVLA . P. S.

—*i.e.*, Pecunia Sua, intimating that he defrayed the cost. In punning allusion to his name, the legs of the seats terminated in a *cow's* cloven hoofs, a *cow's* head forms their upper ornament, and with a *cow*, as we have seen, was decorated the *foculare*. Varro, in his "Treatise on Husbandry," informs us that many of the Roman surnames originated in matters appertaining to a pastoral life; and especially in the animals to whose breeding certain families devoted their particular attention. Thus, the *Porcii* were originally swine-herds; the *Ovini*, sheep-breeders; the *Caprilli* bred goats, the *Equarii* horses, and the *Tauri* bulls. We may conclude, therefore, that the family of the Vacculæ were originally cow-herds, and that the figures of cows so plentifully impressed on all the articles which the patrician presented

---

* Overbeck, "Pompeji," i. 197. Becker, "Gallus," ii. 11, etc.

VIEW OF THE TEPIDARIUM.

to the Thermæ of his native town, are what the heralds call " canting arms"—puns on his own name—as in Rome the family Toria caused a bull to be stamped on their money.*

The tepidarium was embellished in a very splendid and yet not inappropriate manner. The pavement was of white mosaic, with two small borders of black; the ceiling worked in stucco, in low relief, with scattered figures and ornaments of little flying genii delicately designed on medallions, and surrounded with rich borders of foliage—"signis ornatum et jucundis picturis;" the walls glittered with crimson hues; the cornice supported by small Atlas figures, or Telamones,† about two feet high, made of terra-cotta, encrusted with the finest marble. These stand with their backs placed against square pilasters projecting one foot from the wall, and with an interval of one foot three inches and a half between each. They served to divide the chamber into a number of niches, or recesses, in which the garments of those who went into the *sudatorium*, or inner apartment, to undergo the perspiring process, were laid up until their return. Their only clothing is a girdle round the loins; they have been painted flesh colour, with black hair and beards; the moulding of the pedestal, and the basket on their heads, is in imitation of gold; and the pedestal itself, as well as the wall behind them, and the recesses for the bathers' clothes, have been coloured to resemble red porphyry.

Pliny speaks of the tepidarium as "locum laxum et

---

* Pompeii (" Library of Entertaining Knowledge "), L 163.
† From the Greek ταλαω, *I sustain;* or τλῆνω, *I endure.*

hilarem amœnum a meridie illustratum." Both pleasant and cheerful was that of Pompeii, with its radiant colours and bright ornaments; and I can fancy that the gay patrician youth idled here through many an hour of

CEILING OF THE TEPIDARIUM.

sportive converse, discussing the latest fashion in tunics imported from Rome, the last ode recited by the popular poet of the day, or the comparative superiority of the charms of a Lalage, an Amaryllis, or a Neæra. Here, too, on their return from the Calidarium, they were anointed and perfumed in the fashion which I shall afterwards describe.

Into the Calidarium I must now conduct the reader. It answered to the modern vapour-bath. At Pompeii it was a chamber 37 feet long by 17 feet 4 inches broad, with a vault delicately ornamented with stucco mouldings. Its walls are so constructed that a column of heated air encloses it on every side. This is not effected by a multiplicity of flues, but by one universal flue; the said flue being formed by a lining of bricks or tiles strongly connected with the outer wall by iron cramps, yet distant about four inches from it, so as to leave a space where the heated air might ascend from the furnace, and equalize the temperature of the apartment.

ORNAMENTS OF THE TEPIDARIUM.

For a like reason the pavement is hollow. On a flooring of cement (made of lime and pounded bricks) small brick supports are built, 9 inches square, and 1 foot

7 inches high, on which strong tiles, 15 inches square, are carefully laid. The pavement, encrusted with mosaic, rests upon these. The Italians call a flooring of this description *vespajo*, from its resemblance to a wasp's nest.

THE CALIDARIUM.

The calidarium, like the other apartments, is well stuccoed, and painted yellow; a highly-enriched cornice is supported by fluted pilasters, coloured red, and placed at irregular intervals. On one side of the room, in a large semicircular niche, called the *laconicum*, 7 feet wide, and 3 feet 6 inches deep, painted red, and embellished with stucco figures of Cupids and animals, was placed the *labrum*, a vase or tazza of white marble, for washing the face and hands. It was about 5 feet in diameter, but only 7 or 8 inches deep. In the centre the hot water bubbled up through a small tube of brass. It was raised about 3½ feet above the level of the pavement on a round base of lava, stuccoed and coloured red, 5 feet 6 inches in diameter, and within it was engraved the following inscription :— *

CN. MELIOSÆO . CN. F. APRO . M . STAIO .
M. F. RVFO . II . VIR . ITER . ID . LABRVM .
EX. D. D. EX. P. P. F. C. CONSTAT . HS. D.CCL.†

[Cneius Meliosæus Aper, son of Cneius Aper, and Marcus Staius Rufus, son of Marcus Rufus, Duumvirs of Justice for the second time, caused the labrum to be made at the public expense, by order of the Decurions. It cost 750 sestertia (*i.e.*, about £6).]

At the other end of the room, opposite to the labrum, was the hot bath, 4 feet 4 inches wide, 12 feet long, and 1 foot 8 inches deep. It was wholly constructed of marble, with one pipe to introduce the water, and was elevated two steps above the floor. Its brink formed a marble seat 1 foot 4 inches broad, from which the bather descended to a single step, and thence into the hot water. From the shallowness of the basin, it was evidently used as a sitz, or sitting-bath.

* Overbeck, "Pompeji," i. 200.
† I give the Latin in full :—Cnæo Meliosæo Apro, Cnæi Filio Apro, Marco Staio Marci Filio Rufo, Duumviris Iterum, Jure Dicundo Labrum, Ex Decurionum Decreto Ex Pecunia Publica Faciendum Curarunt. Constat Sestertium. D.CCL.

We have seen, then, that the Thermæ at Pompeii consisted of but four principal rooms:—

The *Apodyterium,* or Dressing-Room;
The *Frigidarium,* or Cold-Water Bath;
The *Tepidarium,* or Warming-Room; and
The *Calidarium,* or Vapour and Hot-Water Bath.

It is hardly necessary to say that the great Roman Thermæ were of a more luxurious and complete character. Yet the Pompeian baths are skilfully arranged; space is prudently economized; the parts are so distributed as to offer the bather every facility; the decorations are elegant and profuse; and though the modern architect censures many errors of construction, they form an agreeable and not unsatisfactory whole.

From the frigidarium a narrow passage led to the furnace, upon which were placed three caldrons one above another. These were intrusted to the charge of persons called *fornacatores,* and the furnace was variously named *fornax, ostium furni, propnigeum,* and *præfurnium.*

WOMEN'S BATHS.*

The Women's Baths at Pompeii differ only from the men's in their smaller dimensions and less abundant decoration. They were heated by the same fire, and supplied with water from the same caldrons or boilers. They contained a *frigidarium,* with a cold bath or *natatorium,* a *tepidarium,* and a *calidarium,* with laconicum and hot-water bath. The first chamber measures 25 feet by 12 feet 9 inches. The floor is white mosaic, with a border of black; the walls have been ornamented with

* Sir W. Gell, "Pompeiana," i. 131, *seq.*

alternate red and yellow pilasters, on a blue or black ground. This room was also the undressing or robing-room, and could accommodate ten persons at one time.

The tepidarium is about 20 feet square, and painted yellow, with red pilasters. The calidarium contained some grotesque paintings upon a yellow ground; its pavement was a mosaic of white marble.

We must now direct the reader's attention to what are called, by way of distinction,

THE NEW BATHS,

because excavated as recently as 1858-61. These are on a larger and more magnificent scale than the others, and were probably patronized by the wealthier inhabitants of Pompeii. Their decorations are superb, and their "fittings" luxurious.

The main entrance is from the Street of Abundance, by a wide portal which opens into an ample court or *palæstra*, surrounded by fluted Doric columns with carved capitals. The walls are enriched with a variety of arabesques, paintings, and figures in relief, some of which are in tolerable preservation. On one side stands an oblong basin for a cold bath, from which the bather ascended to either of two graceful halls, whose walls are embellished with vividly-coloured landscapes, and figures of nymphs and damsels carrying baskets.

A door opposite the entrance opens on a *tepidarium*, and on a corridor, from which several private cabinets lead off, each adapted to receive a single bather. On the other side is a *spoliatorium*, with compartments for the reception of clothes, and a square *frigidarium* at one end. From the latter a passage leads into a large square chamber, with hollow walls constructed on the plan already described, for the passage of hot air—this was the *calidarium;* and into another chamber of ample dimensions, the tepidarium, which contains not only the usual bath, square, and wholly made of marble, but a fountain of elegant design. The decorations are everywhere marked by grace and spirit.

The whole side of the Thermæ towards the Street of Stabiæ is occupied with apartments. There are three circular sunk spaces, which probably contained the furnace for the supply of hot water; two *tepidaria*, each fitted up with hollow walls and suspended floors, and with square marble-lined basins; a splendid apodyterium, or *spoliarium*, divided into three portions by as many circular arches, surrounded by marble seats, and richly adorned with stucco relievos of Bacchanals and winged Loves, rosettes, garlands, and fantastic devices. From the apodyterium you pass into a noble *atrium*, also decorated with a profusion of fanciful ornament, and thence into the *palæstra*, or into a circular *frigidarium*, resembling in plan and details the frigidarium of the old Thermæ.

A bronze *foculare*, and seats of bronze, have been discovered here; a sun-dial, with an inscription in Oscan characters, representing that it was raised by Atinius the quæstor from fines levied according to the municipal law; the conduit which supplied the baths with water, and the smaller tubes that distributed it into the various rooms; and also another inscription relative to the erection of the *laconicum*, or vapour-bath, and the *destricta-*

rium, where the operation of scraping by the strigil was performed.*

> C. VLIVS . C. F. P. ANINIVS . C. F. H. V. I. D.
> LACONICVM . ET . DESTRICTARIVM
> FACIVND . ET PORTICVS . ET PALAEST^R
> R. EFICIVNDA . LOCARVNT . EX. D. D. EX.
> EA . PECVNIA . QVOD . EOS . E. LEGE.
> IN LVDOS . AVT . IN MONVMENTO
> CONSVMERE . OPORTVIT . FACIVN.
> COCRARVNT . EIDEMQVE . PROBARV(*NT*).

[Caius Ulius, son of Caius, and Publius Aninius, son of Caius, Duumvirs of Justice, caused to be erected, in obedience to a decree of the Decurions and with the money which, according to law, they were bound to bestow on the games or public monuments, the Laconicum and Destrictarium, and restored the Portico and Palæstra; approving of the same.]

With this description of the Pompeian Thermæ, my readers will probably be content. I now proceed to explain the elaborate bathing processes undergone by their patrons.

On entering the apodyterium, those who took only the cold bath began to undress; they suspended their garments to pegs fastened in the wall, and named *caprarii* from their resemblance to goats' horns, and received, from their own slaves if they were wealthy, or else from the attendants of the Thermæ, loose robes more suited to lavatory operations.

Those who intended to indulge in the hot-bath passed forward into the tepidarium, and, after enjoying for some few minutes its genial voluptuous air, proceeded to unrobe themselves. They were then conducted by slaves called *capsarii* (from *capsa*, the case or bag in which chil-

* Overbeck, "Pompeji," i. 205.

dren carried their books to school), into the *sudatorium*, to undergo the gradual process of the vapour-bath, accompanied by an exhalation of balmy perfumes. This operation over, they were seized by the slaves and subjected to the tender mercies of the strigil, which rasped the skin so as to open its pores very thoroughly. It was not a pleasant process, however skilfully performed, and Suetonius asserts that the Emperor Augustus suffered severely from rough usage. However, it cleansed the skin from the copious perspiration induced by the hot vapour, and gave it a brilliant polish. In the Turkish baths its place is supplied by a bag or glove of camel's hair, which, without pain, peels off the perspiration in large flakes, and leaves the skin wonderfully soft and smooth. Persons of quality carried with them their own apparatus, whence Persius says—

"I, puer, et strigilis Crispi ad balnea defer."[*]
[Go, boy, and carry Crispin's strigils to the baths.]

They were curved at one end like a sickle, and were made of bone, bronze, iron, and silver. Their edge was moderately sharp, and softened by the application of oil. Spartianus relates an amusing anecdote in reference to their use.

"The Emperor Hadrian," he says, "who went to the public baths and bathed with the common people, seeing one day a veteran whom he had formerly known among the Roman troops, rubbing his back and other parts of his body against the marble, inquired of him the reason. The veteran replied that he had no slave to scrape him:

[*] Persius, "Satires," v. 126.

whereupon the emperor gave him a couple of slaves, and a sufficient sum for their maintenance. Another day, several old men, beguiled by the veteran's good fortune, rubbed themselves also against the marble in the emperor's presence. They thought by this means to excite the generosity of Hadrian; but he, perceiving their drift, bade them rub one another."*

Cooled and refreshed, the bathers now passed into the hot-water bath, over which fresh perfumes were freely scattered. This is called the *balineum* by Cicero, *piscina* by Pliny, and *calda lavatio* by Vitruvius. The vapour-bath, as I have previously stated, bore the appellation of the *laconicum*, because it was the custom of the Lacedæmonians to strip and anoint themselves without using warm water after the perspiration produced by the athletic exercises. It is termed *assa* by Cicero, from ἄζω, to dry; because it produced perspiration by means of a dry, hot atmosphere—which Celsus consequently describes as *sudatione assas*, dry sweating.†

Wrapping themselves in their light bathing-robes, the bathers returned from the calidarium to the tepidarium, and prepared to enjoy the special luxury of this series of luxurious ablutions. They were now anointed by slaves (called *unctores* and *aliptæ*) from vials of gold, alabaster, or crystal, filled with the rarest unguents collected from all quarters of the world. Of these the ancients possessed a store which would astonish even a Rimmel or a Houbigant! Among the oils named are the mendesium, megalium, metopium, amaracinum, cyprinum, susinum, nardinum,

* Spartianus, " Hadriani," c. 17.
† Dr. Smith's " Dictionary of Greek and Roman Antiquities," p. 191.

opicatum, and jasmine; and the Emperor Heliogabalus never bathed without oil of saffron or crocum, which was esteemed most precious.* We read also of nitre and aphronitrum in the baths. To these were added all kinds of odoriferous powders called diapasmata. The liquid unguents were named *stymmata*, and the solid, *hedysmata*. Pliny speaks of a regal unguent, originally prepared for a Parthian king, which consisted of no less than twenty-seven ingredients. Some of these articles were very costly, and sold for as much as 400 denarii, or about £14 per lb.†

Common perfumes were sold in little gilt shells, or vessels made of terra-cotta; the more valuable, in bottles (*unguentaria*) of alabaster, onyx, or glass, numbers of which have been discovered at Pompeii. To such an excess did the Romans carry their use, that the Latin satirists are full of invectives against the practice. Martial describes a dandy of those days in bitter lines:—

> "A beau is one who with the nicest care
> In parted locks divides his curling hair;
> One who with balm and cinnamon smells sweet,
> Whose humming lips some Spanish air repeat;
> Whose naked arms are smoothed with pumice-stone,
> And tossed about with graces all his own."‡

While Juvenal, alluding to the employment of cosmetics for the complexion—made into a kind of poultice, which was kept on the face all night and part of the day— asserts that a husband never saw his wife's face at home. But when, attired in all her pomp, she issued forth to receive the applause of the unthinking,—

* Sir W. Gell, "Pompeiana," i. 112.   † Rimmel, "Book of Perfumes," p. 109.
‡ Martial, "Epigramm.," b. lxiii.

"The eclipse then vanishes, and all her face
Is opened and restored to every grace;
The crust removed, her cheeks as smooth as silk
Are polished with a wash of asses' milk;
And should she to the furthest North be sent,
A train of these attend her banishment."*

Our bathers, perfumed and anointed to their hearts' content, may now pass into the portico or palæstra, and enjoy some gentle exercise, previous to their mid-day meal.

The public were informed, by the ringing of a bell placed above the Thermæ, when the water was sufficiently heated, and the baths ready for use. The hour for bathing, according to Pliny, was eight in winter and nine in summer; but this must have frequently varied. Between two and three in the afternoon was, however, considered the most desirable time for the gymnastic exercises of the palæstra and the use of the baths. The Emperor Hadrian forbade all but invalids to enter the Thermæ before two o'clock. This was probably done as a check upon the folly and extravagance of the loungers, who would fain have spent all their days in personal adornment. At a certain hour—five o'clock in the afternoon, according to several authorities—the fires were extinguished and the baths closed. But Alexander Severus, to gratify the Romans in their frenzy for bathing, not only suffered them to be opened at break of day, which had never before been permitted, but provided them with oil-lamps, that they should not be closed too early in the evening on account of the darkness.

They became, in course of time, convenient places for

* Juvenal, "Satires" (Translation by Dryden), Sat. vi.

the congregation of the dissolute and criminal, and the disorders that took place within them could only be suppressed by severe measures. They therefore became unpopular, and as Christianity spread abroad, fell into still greater disrepute; while the magnificent edifices erected by the emperors were destroyed during the barbarian invasions, or suffered to fall into ruinous decay through the lack of public spirit.

A WINE-CART—MEN FILLING THE AMPHORA (FROM A POMPEIAN FRESCO).

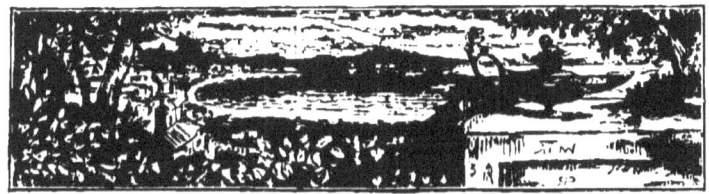

VIII.

Houses of Pompeii.

"The Pompeian houses resembled in some respects the Grecian, but mostly the Roman fashion of domestic architecture. In almost every house there is some difference of detail from the rest, but the principal outline is the same in all. In all you find the hall, the tablinum, and the peristyle, communicating with each other; in all you find the walls richly painted; and in all the evidence of a people fond of the refining elegancies of life. The purity of the taste of the Pompeians in decoration is, however, questionable: they were fond of the gaudiest colours, of fantastic designs; they often painted the lower half of their columns a bright red, leaving the rest uncoloured; and where the garden was small, its wall was frequently tinted to deceive the eye as to its extent, imitating trees, birds, temples, &c., in perspective—a meretricious delusion which the graceful pedantry of Pliny himself adopted, with a complacent pride in its ingenuity."—LORD LYTTON.

ITHERTO we have occupied ourselves with a consideration of the public life of the Pompeians. We have traversed their Forum and their streets; we have visited their theatres and amphitheatres; we have entered their temples; we have witnessed their lavatory processes in the Thermæ; in all observing the revealed evidence of manners, customs, and tastes widely different from our own. We must now pass within their domestic *penetralia*—must cross the thresholds of their private houses—and gather what information we may concerning their home-economy and the conditions of their daily life,—a subject of higher

and more immediate interest, and which we shall, therefore, venture to discuss with some degree of detail.*

Previous to the exhumation of Pompeii, the scholar and the antiquary found it difficult to bring before the labouring imagination a correct presentment of a Roman house. But now it is comparatively easy for even the dullest, by the aid of pen and pencil, to know under what manner of roof, and in what species of "interior," the men of old—to most of us mere historical phantoms, instead of what they should be, flesh and blood realities— passed so much of their stirring lives as they gave up to home.

Home? Did the Romans understand the wealth of domestic happiness, the tender ties, the kindly relationships, the genial interests, which we British strive to express by that one word—Home? Surely not. They lived more in public than we do. They were always *en tenue*, I fancy; always considering in what light they appeared to the great world. There is a fine passage in Catullus:—

> "And every dimple on the cheek of Home
> Shall smile to-night;"

but Catullus writes and feels as a poet, and I believe that the home-feeling in these lines was known but to few of his countrymen. Every well-to-do Roman's house was, in fact, divided into two parts; one intended for the uses of the family, the other for public receptions. This was in some measure due to that Roman institution

---

* See Mazois, "Le Palais de Scaurus;" Becker, "Gallus;" Smith, "Dictionary of Greek and Roman Antiquities," *in locis*.

which permitted every plebeian to choose from among the patricians a patron, whose *client* he thenceforth called himself. The patron was bound to advise, to defend, to assist, to support his client; the client to serve his patron with his life and fortune. Thus, the public rooms of a wealthy and influential patrician were crowded from early dawn with his suitors and retainers, who sought his favour, implored his counsel, or supplicated his charity.

The *public* part, then, included the portico, vestibule, cavædium or atrium, tablinum, alæ, fauces, and others of less importance.

The *private:* the peristyle, cubicula, trichinium, æci, pinacotheca, bibliotheca, thermæ, exedra, and xystus.

Let us now endeavour to build up a house which shall exhibit to our inspection these various apartments.

Having passed the *janua*, or gate, whose folds bent inwards—a Roman could not open his door outwards except by a special law!—and taken note of the inscription at the threshold—Cave Canem (Beware of the dog) —we pass across the vestibule, and through another door into the *atrium*, or hall.*

This, you see, is a large oblong square, surrounded with covered galleries, which rest on pillars of gleaming marble. The side facing you is called the *tablinum*— from tabula, or tabella, a picture—and forms a receptacle for the family archives, the "genealogical tree," the busts, the pictures, and other heirlooms of a long line of an-

* The word *atrium*, according to Varro, is derived from the Atriates, a Tuscan people, who gave the pattern of it. The *cavædium* seems to have been but another word for the same thing: it was the "hollow of the house."—cavum ædium. At first, it was the common room of the whole family, but in due time was given up to public purposes.

cestors. The other sides on the right and left, the *alæ*, are similar but smaller recesses, where strangers and other guests may occasionally be lodged. Yonder narrow passages leading into the interior of the house are appropriately called *fauces*, or jaws. You may remember Virgil's expressive adoption of the term:

"Vestibulum ante ipsum, primisque in faucibus Orci;"

which Conington renders thus:—

"At *Orcus' portals* hold their lair,'—

missing, I venture to think, the peculiar force of the phrase. Before we enter either of these *fauces*, however, we have much to notice still in the atrium.

In the centre of the roof observe an opening, *compluvium*, towards which the roof slopes, so as to eject the rain-water into a cistern in the floor called the *impluvium*. An intolerable nuisance would such an arrangement prove in a wet climate like that of Great Britain; in Italy it was more endurable, but must still have been unsatisfactory. The edge of the compluvium is ornamented with gay tiles (*antefixæ*), moulded with masks and fantastic figures; and the spouts at the corners which carry the water into the impluvium are fashioned into the heads of lions and dogs, which probably suggested the corbels and other grotesque devices of the Gothic architects. Usually the atrium was adorned with fountains, supplied with water from the aqueducts through pipes of lead, and very pleasant on a summer's day was the musical fall of the silvery drops, and the coolness which they diffused through the air. Observe that the opening in the roof is shaded by a gaily-coloured awning, so as to temper the burning heat of Italy's sun, and spread abroad a mellow light. The Roman loved the glow of colours and the beauty of form; so the walls, as you see, are painted with arabesques of fanciful designs, and landscapes seemingly borrowed from Fairyland, each set round with a border of marble slabs of the rarest and most costly kinds. The pavement is enriched with mosaics, arranged in exquisite geometrical patterns.

Let us now pass into the private portion of the house, and leave behind us the hum of the noisy clients. Through the tablinum we enter the *peristyle*, which reminds us at once, in its general arrangement, of the atrium. It is a court, open to the sapphire sky in the middle, and surrounded by a bright and stately colonnade. Its owner has embellished the area with parterres of blooming flowers and clumps of glossy evergreens, so that it is rather what the Romans call a *xystus* than a peristyle. In shape it is an oblong.

Turning aside from the *cubicula*, or bed-chambers, which, indeed, are low and insignificant, and entirely deficient in what we now understand as comfort, we next proceed to inspect the *triclinium*, or dining-room, so named from the three couches which encompassed the table on three sides, leaving the fourth open to the attendants. This is the most sumptuously decorated apartment in the house; for our Romans, like aldermen and common-councilmen, loved the pleasures of the table, and failed not to display the utmost magnificence in everything connected with their entertainments. In a wealthy patrician's house were frequently several triclinia. Every school-boy knows the story of the sumptuous Lucullus, who had a separate triclinium for each style of banquet, and who, having invited Pompey and Cicero to a private supper, merely despatched a message to his servants that he would sup in the hall called Apollo, to ensure the preparation of an entertainment worth 50,000 denarii (about £1600). The ceiling was sometimes contrived to open, and admit of the descent of a second course, with showers of choice blossoms and a spray of perfumed waters, while rope-dancers, or *funambuli*, performed their wondrous feats over the heads of the company.

The triclinium,* into which we have just entered, is twice as long as it is broad, and divided, as it were, into two parts—the upper occupied by the table and the couches, the lower left empty for the accommodation of servants and spectators. Around the former the walls, up to a certain height, are hung with valuable tapestry. It was the fall of these hangings, the classical student will remember, caused dire confusion at that supper of Nasidienus' to which Horace was invited:—

"Interea suspensa graves aulæa ruinas
In patinam fecere; trahentia pulveris atri
Quantum non Aquilo Campanis excitat agris,"— †

when they filled the chamber with such a cloud of black dust as not even the east wind stirs up on the plains of Campania! The decorations of the remainder of the room are handsome, and appropriate to its destination: garlands, mingled with the trailing ivy and graceful vine,

* The following description is adapted in the main from the elaborate and exhaustive work of Mazois, "Le Palais de Scaurus," c. ix.
† Horace, "Satires," bk. ii., s. 8, L 54-56.

divide the walls into compartments, edged round with fanciful borders; in the centre of each, touched with the

FEMALE CENTAUR AND BACCHANTE (FROM A POMPEIAN FRESCO).

painter's liveliest skill, young fawns are frisking, or Centaurs and half-naked Bacchanals, riding, sporting, danc-

MALE CENTAUR AND BACCHANTE (FROM A POMPEIAN FRESCO).

ing, carrying thyrsi, vases, goblets, and other festal appurtenances. A large frieze above the columns is set out in twelve compartments; each is surmounted by one of the signs of the zodiac, and contains a painting of the viands in highest season in that particular month of the year: thus, under Sagittarius, or December, you see shrimps, shell-fish, and birds of passage; to Capricornus, or January, belong lobsters, sea-fish, wild boar, and game; and to Aquarius, or February, pigeons, water-rails, ducks, and plovers.

Bronze lamps, manufactured at Ægina, and costing from £200 to £400 a-piece, suspended from chains of the same metal, as in Dido's regal hall—

> " From the gilt roof hang cressets bright,
> And flambeau-fires put out the light "—

or raised on richly wrought candelabra, stream through the room a brilliant light. Slaves, whose peculiar charge it is to tend them, trim the wicks, and from time to time supply the necessary oil.

The table, made of citron wood from the extremity of Mauritania, more precious than gold, rests upon an ivory pedestal, and is covered by a plateau of solid silver, chased and carved. The couches, which will accommodate thirty guests, are made of bronze, overlaid with rich ornamental work in silver, gold, and tortoise-shell. The mattresses, of Gallic wool, are dyed purple; the luxurious cushions, fit for Venus herself to repose upon, are covered with superb stuffs, embroidered in threads of gold. Our host informs us that they were woven in the looms of Babylon, and cost four millions of sesterces (about £32,000).

Now observe the mosaic pavement. You will see that

it represents all the fragments of a feast, as if they had fallen in common course on the floor. At the first glance you would suppose the room has not been swept since the last meal; and hence it is called ἀθάρωτος ϋικος, the unswept saloon. Large vases of Corinthian brass glitter at the end of the hall. And now, while we stand admiring their graceful shape, some young slaves enter, and strew over the polished pavement sawdust dyed with saffron and vermilion, and mingled with a brilliant powder made from the lapis specularis, or talc.

Here we may close our imaginary visit to a Roman house, and content ourselves with a brief description of its remaining chambers.

The *Oeci*, from the Greek οἶκος, were large halls or saloons, whose design was borrowed from the Greeks, like their name. They resembled the triclinia, but having columns, were more spacious. Four kinds are described by Vitruvius:—The tetrastyle, whose roof was supported by four pillars; the Corinthian, with but one row of columns, which sustained the architrave, cornice, and a vaulted roof; the more splendid Egyptian, resembling a basilica, with a gallery resting on pillars, open to the sky, and surrounding the room, so as to afford a pleasant promenade; and the Cyzicene, intended only for summer use. The latter generally opened upon a flower-garden through folding-doors.

The *Exedræ* bore a double signification. They were either seats intended to contain a number of persons, or spacious rooms for conversation and other social purposes. In the Thermæ, or public baths, the same term was applied to the semicircular apartments set aside for the resort of philosophers.

The Pinacotheca, or picture-gallery, was devoted, as its name implies, to the reception of paintings and statues. It was of ample size, and faced the north, in order that the light might be equable, and not too strong.

AN ANCIENT GALLEY (FROM A POMPEIAN FRESCO).

Only a small room was required for the Bibliotheca, or library. The rolls (volumina) which made up the books of the Romans were easily arranged in a very limited space. It was the fashion, however, to set aside a bibliotheca in every opulent house, though its owner might be scarcely able to read the titles of his manuscripts. Cases containing the rolls were placed around the walls, and at suitable points statues of Minerva and the Muses, and busts and portraits of eminent personages, were set up. The cases were variously called *armaria, loculamenta, foruli,* or *nidi.*

Of the Balneæ, or baths, frequently found attached to private houses, the arrangements were similar, though necessarily on a smaller scale, to those which obtained in the public institutions.

Such were the chief apartments of a Roman house.

They were on the ground-floor; the upper stories being generally appropriated to the slaves, freedmen, and lower branches of the family. We must except, however, the terrace upon the top of all (*solarium*), a favourite promenade and place of resort, adorned with rare flowers and shrubs planted in beds of mould, and with statues, sparkling fountains, and garlanded trellises, under which the evening meal might at pleasure be taken. In houses of different classes a different distribution of rooms was found. Some possessed several triclinia; some had neither bibliotheca nor pinacotheca : as in modern times, all depended upon the wealth and taste of the owner. To men of moderate fortune, says Vitruvius,* magnificent vestibules, and tablina, and atria, are needless, for they attend upon persons of higher rank instead of entertaining numerous visitors at home. Those who dispose of their rural produce require shops and stables at the entrances of their houses, granaries and storehouses below, and other arrangements appertaining rather to use than to beauty. The houses of money-lenders, and of those who farm the revenue, should be on a handsome scale, and secure against attacks. Lawyers and public speakers require more elegant accommodation, and apartments capable of receiving a large assemblage. For patricians who hold the offices and honours of the state, and who are consequently exposed to a crowd of suitors, regal vestibules, lofty halls, and ample peristyles are indispensable; with leafy plantations, and extensive walks, laid out with every attention to magnificence. They should also have libraries, picture-galleries, and

* Vitruvius, " De Architectura," vi. 7, 8.

basilicæ ordered upon the same scale as public buildings, for in their mansions both public business and affairs are frequently discussed and determined.

The Roman houses were very sparingly decorated. Neither gold nor silver was generally employed, nor those luxuries in cabinet-work and furniture which are so prized by the moderns. Their mosaic pavements, however, were of exquisite beauty. The walls were adorned with a stucco of great excellence, equally adapted to receive pictorial embellishment or to be modelled into bas-reliefs. This stucco was called *albarium*, from its whiteness, or *opus marmoratum*, from its resemblance to marble. It seems to have been made of calcined gypsum (plaster of Paris), mixed with pulverized stone, and, in the more expensive sort, with powdered marble. A wall thus prepared was divided by the artist into rectangular compartments, which he filled with free and fanciful designs of landscapes, buildings, animals, gardens, or ideal subjects.*

With these introductory remarks, I proceed to an examination of some of the houses of Pompeii.

THE HOUSE OF THE TRAGIC POET. †

This elegant mansion, for so it would be termed in Mayfair or Belgravia, was discovered in 1824, when it received the misnomer by which it is still popularly dis-

---

* Compare Mazois, " Le Palais de Scaurus ;" Becker, "Gallus ;" and " Pompeii," in the Library of Entertaining Knowledge.

† To prevent a recurrence of unnecessary references, I may state at the outset that my description is based upon the works of Overbeck, Mazois, Sir William Gell, Dr. Dyer, and the volumes of the Library of Entertaining Knowledge entitled " Pompeii."

HOUSE OF THE TRAGIC POET.

THE VESTIBULE.

tinguished, from a painting extant upon its walls. It is situated in the Street of the Baths, in the same "insula," or block, that contains the Fullonica and Houses of the Fountains. When first excavated, it attracted the admiration of every visitor from the beauty and richness of its decorations. Most of these have been removed to the Museum at Naples; and in the following description, therefore, the reader must understand me to speak of it as it *was*, not as it *is*.

The doors, turning upon pivots received in two brass sockets let into the marble threshold, admit us within a long and narrow VESTIBULE, where the first object which greets the eye is the somewhat alarming one of a large and fierce dog preparing to spring upon the incautious visitor. Look closer, however, and you perceive it is but a device wrought on the pavement in mosaic, with the well-known inscription beneath of

BEWARE OF THE DOG!

Cave Canem (Beware of the dog)

An inscription, as we learn from a passage in Petronius Arbiter, not unfrequently placed at the entrance of Roman houses.

The vestibule is about 6 feet wide, and nearly 30 feet long. On either side lies a chamber of moderate dimensions, which may have been set apart for the reception of ordinary visitors, or have been occupied by the servants of the family. At all events, I cannot agree with those authorities who would convert them into shops.

Advancing up the vestibule, and drawing aside a rich curtain, we enter the ATRIUM, which measures about 28 feet by 20. It is provided as usual with an *impluvium* and a *puteal*. The floor is prettily paved with white tesseræ, spotted at intervals with black; and round the impluvium is a well-executed pattern, also in black. The walls glow with admirable paintings,—bright in colour, powerful in expression. Their subjects, and those of the adjacent chambers, occur in the following order:— Marriage of Peleus and Thetis—also called, the Interview of Thetis and Jupiter; Parting of Achilles and Briseis; painting, much decayed, supposed to represent the Departure of Chryseis; Battle of the Amazons; Fall of Icarus; Venus Anadyomene; Sacrifice of Iphigenia; Leda and Tyndareus; Thesus and Ariadne; Cupid.

Whoever may have been the owner of this house, he must have possessed a poet's taste, to judge from this selection of Homeric and mythological themes for the painter's brush.

The subject of the first picture is doubtful. Three figures are represented; one, a man of middle age, seated, and in the act of taking the left arm of the second, a female, who extends it in no amiable mood. A winged figure, standing behind her, seems to urge her to put forward her right hand. At Peleus' feet sit three children; the offspring, it may be, of his marriage with Antigone.

The second picture, one of remarkable merit, describes Achilles delivering his beautiful handmaiden, Briseis, to the heralds, Talthybius and Eurybates, charged with her escort to Agamemnon. It is founded on a well-known

ACHILLES DELIVERS BRISEIS TO THE HERALDS OF AJAX.

passage in the first book of the Iliad. The Greeks having taken two beautiful captives, Chryseis and Briseis, allotted the former to Agamemnon, the latter to Achilles. Chryses, the priest of Apollo, then betook himself to the Greek camp before Troy, to ransom his daughter, but was injuriously treated by Agamemnon, and dismissed with great contumely. Apollo thereupon revenged his insulted servant by inflicting a pestilence on the Greeks, who were informed by their soothsayer, Calchas, that it could only be stayed by the restoration of Chryseis to her father. The king was accordingly constrained to deliver up his prize, but he avenged himself by seizing on Briseis, who had been allotted to Achilles.

The artist shows us the bust of the illustrious Greek warrior, who sits in the centre—his eyes glowing with indignation, and his haughty brow contracted in the effort to restrain his emotion. His faithful ·Patrocles, with his back towards the spectator, leads in from the left the lovely Briseis, clothed in a long flowing veil, and endeavouring to check the gathering tears. Her face is beautiful, and, not to dwell upon the arch vivacity of her eyes, it is evident that "the voluptuous pouting of her ruby lips" was imagined by the painter as one of her most charming attributes.

HEAD OF ACHILLES (FROM GELL).

The heralds are placed on the right of Achilles; and behind a breast-high drapery, which partitions off the tent, stand several warriors with golden shields and plumed helms.

" With reluctant steps they passed
Along the margin of the watery waste,

> Till to the tents and ships they came, where lay
> The warlike myrmidons. Their chief they found
> Sitting beside his tent and dark-ribbed ship.
> Achilles marked their coming, not well pleased:
> With troubled look, and awe-struck, by the king
> They stood, nor dared accost him; but himself
> Divined their errand, and addressed them thus:
>   'Welcome, ye messengers of gods and men!
> Heralds! approach in safety; not with you,
> But with Atrides is my just offence,
> Who for the fair Briseis sends you here.
> Go, then, Patroclus, bring the maiden forth,
> And give her to their hands.' . . . .
>   He spoke: obedient to his friend and chief,
> Patroclus led the fair Briseis forth,
> And gave her to their hands; they to the ships
> Retraced their steps, and with them the fair girl
> Reluctant went."*

The third picture is to the left of the door of the cubiculum. It is so much defaced that one cannot decide with any certainty upon its subject, but it may probably be regarded as a continuation of the Homeric narrative, and as representing the restoration of Chryseis to her father.

> "Whereat Atrides full of fury rose,
> And uttered threats, which he hath now fulfilled.
> For Chryses' daughter to her native land
> In a swift-sailing ship the keen-eyed Greeks
> Have sent, with costly offerings to the god."

Opposite to the picture of Achilles and Briseis was once a representation of the Fall of Icarus. The waxen wings with which he had essayed his daring flight had melted, and he was descending prone into the sea; there, however, to be rescued from destruction by a winged sea-god riding on a dolphin.

The colouring of the Venus Anadyomene is described

* Homer, "Iliad," bk. i, translated by Earl of Derby.

as reminding the critic in its glow and vividness of the radiant hues which illumine the canvas of Titian. At the feet of the goddess lies a dove with a myrtle-branch in her beak.

The Battle of the Amazons forms the subject of a broad frieze in a small chamber to the left of the atrium. The figures are sketched with wonderful freedom—some in chariots, some on horseback, all armed with bows, as well as with shields and battle-axes. They are clad in blue, green, and purple draperies, and depicted in violent action; some pursuing the fugitive Greeks, others borne down by their stronger opponents. "An Amazon, whose horse is falling, and who, though wounded herself, yet retains her seat, is a masterpiece of attitude, however negligently the picture may be touched."*

We now come to the TABLINUM, across which, at either end, hang rich draperies of Tyrian purple, half withdrawn. The most notable thing in it is a mosaic representing the distribution of masks to a chorus.

Sir William Gell describes it as the best and largest mosaic, deserving the name of a picture, which has yet been discovered. It represents, on a black ground, an Ionic colonnade decorated with shields, festoons, and fillets, in front of which an aged choragus, seated, is apportioning the proper masks and costumes to his various performers. Two youths on the left seem already provided with a scanty savage dress of goat-skins; a person near the centre plays the double flute, while his habit is adjusted by an attendant behind, and another is

---

* Sir W. Gell, "Pompeiana," Second Series, i. 164.

pulling over the head of a comic actor a species of shirt adapted to his character.

The dresses are mostly white, but the flute-player's robe is embroidered with purple; her garland, flutes, and mouth-band (*capistrum*), with most of the ornaments, are coloured gold. The masks are painted to imitate life, and with different hair and complexions, according to the age and character to be represented.

The tablinum also contains the picture of a poet reading, which originally gave to the house the name which it now bears. In the foreground sits the poet, reading from a roll to two auditors, one male, the other female, all seated. Behind a species of partition appear Apollo and the Muse; and, on the other side of the painting, a woman and an old man. Some authorities would identify the poet with Plautus, because he is represented with a dark skin, like a slave. Others consider him to be one of the Athenians captured at Syracuse, who, according to Thucydides, mitigated the harshness of their captivity in consequence of the pleasure they afforded their masters by repeating the verses of Euripides. And others, with more probability, conjecture that the painting celebrates a famous incident in the life of Virgil, who, when reciting the Æneid to Augustus and Octavia, moved the latter to tears by the beautiful eulogium on the dead Marcellus. The only objection to this hypothesis is the nudity of both the poet and the emperor.*

The walls of this apartment are embellished with an abundance of fantastic ornament: pillars with human heads for capitals, swans, goats, lions, and winged harpies

---
* Sir W. Gell, "Pompeiana," ii. 113.

The peristyle, which we enter from the tablinum, consists of a small court, anciently blooming with flowers and foliage, and enclosed by seven Doric columns, whose lower portion, and the podium on which they stand, were painted red. The wall beyond is painted blue, to imitate the sky, while below it the tops of trees rise above a parapet, so as to afford the idea of a rural landscape. At the left angle stands a small ædicula, or shrine, in which probably stood a statue, found near the spot, representing a faun carrying flowers and fruits. A railing ran between the pillars, to prevent the garden from being injured by heedless feet.

On the left side are two cubicula, one of which has been called the library, from a circular painting with books and implements for writing; the other contains two pictures, one of Venus and Cupid fishing, the other of Ariadne. The latter is seen awakening from the fatal slumber during which Theseus had deserted her. The vessel that bears away her fugitive lover is careering merrily over the azure sea.

At the end of the right side of the colonnade is figured the Sacrifice of Iphigenia. Does the reader remember the touching story? Her father, Agamemnon, having slain unwittingly a favourite deer belonging to Diana, the soothsayer Calchas declares that the wrath of the goddess can only be appeased by the sacrifice of Iphigenia. She was bound to the altar, and Calchas—as the Pompeian painting shows—preparing to strike the fatal blow, when the goddess, relenting, bore her in a cloud to Tauris, and made her a priestess in her temple. This was a favourite theme with the painters of antiquity, and the reader will recollect that Timanthes,* unable to give fitting expression to the father's intense agony, solved the difficulty by covering his head with a cloak. The same expedient is adopted in the Pompeian picture. Above, Diana appears in the clouds, with the hind which was to fill Iphigenia's place as a victim.

SACRIFICE OF IPHIGENIA.

At the side of this fresco we enter a room near twenty feet square, and of considerable height, which, from a painting on one of its walls, is called the Triclinium, or the Chamber of Leda. This design, representing Leda

* Polygnotus of Thasos, who lived in the fifth century B.C., had also painted the same subject, and Euripides imagined it, with the same circumstances.

presenting her infant progeny* to Tyndareus, is one of the most admirable productions of ancient art, both as regards its conception, its composition, and its colouring. Thorwaldsen, the Danish sculptor, regarded it with the greatest admiration. There is also a fine painting of a beautiful Cupid, leaning on the knees of Venus, to whom Adonis seems to be addressing himself; and another version of the popular story of Ariadne. Here she is seen asleep; her head surrounded with a blue *nimbus*, or glory, which, in all ancient pictures, distinguishes a god-like personage, and probably suggested to the early Christian painters the coronas with which they encircled their saints. Theseus, who has just quitted her, is in the act of stepping on board his galley, while Minerva appears in the air to guide his course and excuse his perfidy.

On the plinth is represented, with much force and truth, a combat between a lion and two centaurs. The animal is so accurately delineated, that one might suppose Pompeii to have boasted of a Sir Edwin Landseer!

The flooring is of mosaic, very gracefully arranged, and the lower part of the wall was gaily decorated with garlands, sea-horses, and other devices.

Such is a general account of the House of the Tragic Poet. Could we re-create it, in all the novel splendour of its pictured walls, its blooming garden, its vases and statues, and its costly tapestries, the reader would admit that the ancients well knew how to please the eye and charm the refined taste—how to throw over their domestic life the grace, elegance, and attractiveness of art— how to adorn their houses with things of beauty, which

* Pollux, Helen, and Castor.

stimulated the imagination and furnished constant subjects of contemplation to the thoughtful mind.*

On the opposite side of the street to the poet's mansion stands the

HOUSE OF CERES,

also called the *House of the Bacchantes*, and of *Zephyrus
and Flora*. It received the latter appellation in allusion
to a large picture supposed to represent the marriage of
the goddess of flowers with the " silky, soft Favonius."†
Others, however, have seen in the same design an embodiment of the dream of Rhea; and all that can be safely
said of it is, that it shows a winged figure, conducted by
Cupids, approaching a sleeping maiden on the ground.
Whether the figure be indeed

"The frolic wind that breathes the spring,"

must be left to the spectator's imagination.

From the height and appearance of the walls, it is
conjectured that this house was two stories high. The
atrium was gorgeously decorated, and in the palmy days
of Pompeii must have presented a very radiant aspect.
Its painted walls had been touched by the hand of no
insignificant artist. Here Jupiter sat in his curule chair,
his mighty brow resting on his right hand, while in his
left he held the golden sceptre of majesty. The eagle
crouched at his feet. His head was surrounded with a

* A mass of curious and interesting relics was discovered in this house, including necklaces and bracelets of gold, ear-rings of pearls, a ring of onyx, kitchen
utensils, silver and brass coins, a vase for oil, a tripod, glass decanters, iron
hatchets and hammers, fifty-six terra-cotta lamps, and a head of Hermes in
giallo antico. From the nature of these articles, it has been supposed that the
house belonged to a silversmith. If so, "the man had a taste!"

† Now in the Museum at Naples.

nimbus or glory. The throne and footstool were of gold, ornamented with precious stones; the former partly covered with green cloth. The god's mantle was violet-hued, and lined with azure. Everywhere colour was distributed with boldness, but not the less with judgment, and the fancy of an original artist shone conspicuous in each fair painting.

A cistern in front of the impluvium was decorated with coarse mosaics, representing winged sphinxes, a river, and two large masks.

Returning to what we may call the poet's side of the street, we pass on to the

HOUSES OF THE FOUNTAINS.

The first of these is of considerable dimensions. You approach it from the Street of the Mercuries by a handsome and lofty portal, and enter an atrium of peculiarly imposing character. It measures not less than 50 feet by 40, with the usual arrangement of alæ and tablinum. The peristyle only contains three Corinthian columns of indifferent design; but it possesses a fountain, which, if not of great beauty, is remarkable for its curious construction. Thus, it is completely incrusted with a species of mosaic, consisting of vitrified tesseræ of different colours, but mostly blue. The chief divisions of the patterns and borders are formed by real shells; nearly all the ornaments have an appropriate meaning, such as aquatic plants and birds. The general outline of the fountain is a semicircular alcove, surmounted by a pediment; the water trickling from a mosaic mask, and bubbling over a small flight of steps, to be received in a species of raised basin. In front, a round column pierced for a pipe seems to have been intended for a *jet d'eau*. On each side of the alcove grins a comic mask, hollowed out, it has been conjectured, to receive lights, which at night would have a fantastic, nay, even an eery effect.

The *House of the Small Fountain* is not of inferior interest. The tablinum is enriched with a lively painting of Cupid milking Goats. The peristyle contains a fountain very similar, both in design and construction, to that already noticed. It presents the same kind of alcove, surmounted by a pediment, whose breadth is 7 feet, and whose height 7 feet 7 inches. The face projects 5 feet from the wall. Formerly a little bronze fisherman angled in the piscina, which had in its centre a small pedestal for a bird spouting water, but both fisherman and bird have been removed to the Naples Museum. And not only these, but the caryatid and sleeping fisherman—both in marble—which formerly ornamented either side of the alcove. How grateful must have been the murmuring lapse of the fountain on a hot summer noon, and beneath a cloudless Italian sky, when the sunshine streamed into the pillared peristyle, and flung a golden lustre on its pictured walls! Alas! it will never more gleam and sparkle with iris-like hues! Never again will its song fall tenderly on the listening ear!

Two rooms—one called a triclinium; the other an exedra, or hall for company—open into the portico. The former is painted in imitation of brick-work; the latter enriched with vivid pictures of game and the chase. Around the peristyle and atrium lie the usual cubicula, or sleeping-rooms. As there are two staircases, this house must have had an upper story; and it should be noted that it possesses a second entrance, affording access to the peristyle and private apartments without passing through the atrium.

At the corner of this mansion, in the Street of Mercuries, is the Fountain of Mercury, so called from its rude sculpture of the head and caduceus of the god. On an opposite wall the same nefarious deity is represented running away with a stolen purse; scarcely an incentive, one would think, to public morality. But morality was not very religiously considered in luxurious Pompeii.

We turn from the beautiful to the useful; from the gaily adorned houses of Pompeian patricians to the depôt and storehouse of a Pompeian tradesman. Between the House of the Dramatic Poet and the Houses of the Fountains stands the

FULLONICA,*

or establishment for fulling and scouring cloth. As wool was the only material employed for dresses at this period, and from its nature required constant purification, the fuller's trade was one of great importance. Its different processes are illustrated with much graphic effect on the walls of the Fullonica, and may be briefly described.

The primary operation was that of washing, which was done in vats, the cloth being well worked and trodden by the fuller's feet, in water mixed with fuller's earth or some detergent clay.

The cloth was then dried, and afterwards brushed and

* Sir W. Gell, " Pompeiana," i. 189; ii. 122-125.

carded, to raise the nap; at first with thin metal cards, and next with thistles. A plant called teazle is still extensively cultivated in England for the same purpose. The fumigating process followed, sulphur being employed; and the cloth was afterwards bleached in the sun by throwing water repeatedly upon it, while spread out on gratings.

FULLERS AT WORK.

In one of the pictures a man is seen carrying a bleaching-frame and a pot to hold sulphur; the frame has a suspicious resemblance to a modern lady's crinoline! The owl sitting upon it would seem to indicate that the establishment was under the patronage of Minerva, unless it was the portrait of some favourite bird of the owner.

The last operation was that of pressing. The press consisted of two upright timbers, united by another below, and a fourth above. From the upper horizontal beam two perpendicular screws are brought to bear on a thick board, which presses down several pieces of cloth. The screws are turned by horizontal pins or levers, which are run through them; and the whole is adorned with three little festoons of drapery.

ANCIENT FULLERS.

The court of the Fullonica measures 65 feet by 22 feet 6 inches. In the portico was found a large circular vase or jar, which had been broken across the centre horizontally, and fastened together in a peculiarly careful manner with metal wire, seeming to indicate that such vases, though of common red clay—mere pipkins, which an English peasant-woman would despise—must have borne a high price at Pompeii.

The west end of the court is entirely filled up with four large square vats, or tanks, built of solid masonry and lined with stucco. They measure above 7 feet in depth, and it required a little flight of steps to enable the fuller to examine them. The water seems to have passed from one into the other *seriatim;* and the portico on the north side retains the vestiges of six or seven smaller basins, used for washing lighter articles, or to hold the different mixtures which prepared the cloth for receiving a new colour.

At the east end stood a fountain, or *jet d'eau*, of peculiarly graceful design.

The next mansion to which I shall conduct the reader is

THE HOUSE OF HOLCONIUS,

situated at the corner of the Street of the Theatres and the Street of the Holconii, its principal entrance being in the latter.

It will be needless, however, to enter into a description of its interior arrangements, which correspond with those of other Pompeian mansions. It has its peristyle, its tablinum, its atrium, its cubicula. The floor of the tablinum is of pounded brick, cased over with a thin layer of marble.* Most of the paintings have vanished, but you may still recognize a sketch of the favourite myth of Diana wooing Endymion on the Latmian hill, and another of Leda with three children seated in a nest. Several skeletons were discovered in various parts of the building; notably, one of a female, supposed to be the mistress of the house, who, while endeavouring to escape with a small casket of her most valued treasures, was overtaken by the destructive vapour.

The *xystus*, or flower-garden, which embellished the pillared peristyle, contained in its centre a small *piscina*, or basin, between six and seven feet deep, and a marble pedestal therein, for the supply of a *jet d'eau*. Another fountain, on the further side of the garden, is of more

* Overbeck, " Pompeji," i. 269, *sqq*.

original design; a boy, sculptured in pure white marble, holds under one arm a swan, and in the other a vase, from which the water falls in a mimic cascade down a small flight of steps. Holconius, I fancy, must have possessed an ear for music and an eye for colour, since bright melodious jets of water gushed from several of the columns at a height of about four feet from the ground, and fell into a broad channel carried round the flower-beds. In the piscina-walls may be seen eight iron hooks, which were probably designed to keep fruit and other articles cool by suspending them in the fresh cold running water.

The walls of the peristyle are painted black, but relieved by small decorated designs of game and other articles of food, the lower border being appropriated to aquatic plants and water-fowl; and the general effect being very gay and pleasing. A *graffite* was found scrawled on one side to this effect: "July 7th, lard 200 lbs., garlic 250 bundles;" referring, I suppose, to the quantity sold or purchased on that particular day.

One of the *cubicula*, or bed-chambers, is handsomely decorated; the walls, painted in red and yellow, are covered with architectural designs, and with bold rough sketches of sea-nymphs riding on the back of Tritons and ocean-monsters. An *exedra*, or ante-room, paved with black and white marble, contains a small central *impluvium*, and several pictures of meritorious execution: the Three Muses, Bacchus and his "merry crew" discovering Ariadne, Silenus supporting a Hermaphrodite, and Narcissus contemplating his handsome person in the mirror of a fountain.

Dr. Dyer, in a recent work, has described the " Bacchus

BACCHUS AND ARIADNE: FRESCO DISCOVERED AT POMPEII.

and Ariadne" very minutely,* and as the subject was a favourite one with Pompeian artists, I borrow his description.

* Dr. Dyer, " Ruins of Pompeii," pp. 80, 81.

Bacchus, after his arrival at Naxos, finds Ariadne sunk in a profound slumber. Her face is hid in the pillows; over her head stands Sleep, with outspread wings, as if to take his departure, and bearing in his left hand a torch reversed, a symbol common to him with his brother Death. A young faun lifts the sheet, or veil, in which Ariadne is enveloped, in an attitude expressive of surprise at her beauty, and looks earnestly at the god, as if to discover what impression it makes on him. Bacchus, crowned with ivy and berries, clothed in a short tunic and flowing pallium, having on his legs rich buskins, and holding in his right hand the thyrsus bound with a fillet, appears to be approaching slowly and cautiously, for fear that he should awake the nymph. Meanwhile, a Bacchante in the background raises her tambourine, and seems to strike it strongly, as if summoning the Bacchic troop to descend from the mountains. At the head of these marches Silenus, also crowned with ivy, and supporting his footsteps with a long knotted staff. He is followed by a Faun playing on the double flute, and by eight Bacchantes. On a part of the mountain to the left, from which springs a tree, another Bacchante and Faun are looking on the scene below.

Such was the mode of treatment adopted by ancient artists.

The next Pompeian mansion to which I shall introduce the reader is entitled the

HOUSE OF PANSA,

from the words *Pansam. ÆD.*, painted in red near the principal entrance. Mazois, however, very justly re-

ATRIUM OF THE HOUSE OF PANSA.

marks, that as the name is in the accusative, it is evidently one of those eulogistic inscriptions in honour of an ædile, or some other high officer, so common in Pompeii, and is not in itself any evidence that the house in question belonged to Pansa. It will be convenient, nevertheless, to preserve the common appellation.

This house occupies an entire *insula*, or block; in other words, it is completely surrounded by streets. It is situated in one of the best situations in the town, close to the Thermæ, and near the Forum. Including the garden, which occupies a third of the whole length, its area is about 300 feet by 100; part of this, however, according to the Pompeian custom, is apportioned to shops belonging to the owner, and rented by various tradesmen. Three of these were occupied by bakers.

Internally, we find the mansion contains a vestibule; an atrium, with impluvium; the usual alæ, or wings; open tablinum; peristyle; apartments for visitors on each side of the atrium; œcus, or triclinium, for use in winter; a large triclinium; open court; cubicula; a large summer œcus, opening on the garden; kitchen; a servants' hall; a cabinet; and two-storied portico. In arrangement and extent, it is the most noticeable house in Pompeii.*

It would be tedious to describe in detail every apartment, since the reader must now have a reasonably accurate idea of the domestic arrangements of the ancients. My remarks will therefore be limited to objects of special interest. The peristyle was unusually spacious, measuring about 65 feet by 50. An arcade ran around it, 16

* Overbeck, "Pompeji," i. 296, *sqq.*; "Pompeii" (Lib. Enter. KnowL), ii. 98, *sqq.*

feet wide, formed by sixteen Ionic columns of about the same height. In the kitchen was found a curious religious painting, illustrative of the worship offered to the *Lares domestici*, under whose protection the provisions, and all the culinary utensils, were placed. In the centre is a sacrifice in honour of these deities, who are represented in the usual form of two immense serpents brooding over an altar. The female in the middle of the sacrificial group holds a cornucopia, and each of the males holds a small vase in one hand, and a horn in the other. Their heads are surrounded with a species of nimbus. Different kinds of food are represented on either side of the picture; fish, a group of small birds, a large boar, an eel, a boar's head, a joint of pork, and a few cakes. "The execution," says one authority, "is coarse and careless in the extreme, yet there is a spirit and freedom of touch which has hit off the character of the objects represented, and forbids us to impute the negligence displayed to incapacity."

The kitchen also contains a stove for stews, a species of flat ladle pierced with holes, a knife, a strainer, and a frying-pan with some spherical cavities, which seems to have been employed in cooking eggs.

Several paintings were found in Pansa's house, of which the most meritorious is said to have represented Jupiter wooing Danae in a shower of gold. Skeletons were also discovered, some of them recognized for females by their gold ear-rings; vessels of silver, a vase finely carved with bas-reliefs, and vessels of bronze, glass, and terra-cotta. The garden consisted, we are told, of a number of straight parallel beds, divided by narrow paths which gave access to them for horticultural purposes, but with no walks suitable for exercise, except the portico which adjoins the house.

Inferior in size to the mansion named after Pansa, but second to none in grace and beauty of decoration, is the

HOUSE OF SALLUST,

situated in the Street of Herculaneum and the Via Domitiana. It was formerly called the *House of Actæon*, from a fresco on the wall of the women's *atrium;* and owes its present appellation to an inscription, C. SALLUST. M. F., painted on the outer wall. It occupies an area of about forty square yards, and is surrounded on three sides by streets, the front of the ground floor being occupied by shops. The entrance doorway is flanked by pilasters with lava capitals, one of which represents Silenus teaching a young Faun to play the pastoral pipe. The atrium contains the usual impluvium, and, beyond it, a small altar for the worship of the household gods. In the centre of the basin formerly stood a bronze hind, through whose mouth flowed a stream of water. It bore a figure of Hercules upon its back. The walls of the atrium and tablinum are stuccoed in large raised panels painted of different and strongly-contrasting colours. The floor was of red cement, inlaid with pieces of white marble.

Passing through the tablinum, we enter the portico of the xystus, or garden, "a spot small in extent, but full of ornament and beauty." The portico, says an exact authority, is composed of columns, fluted and corded, the lower portion of them painted blue, without pedestals, yet approaching to the Roman rather than to the Grecian Doric. From the portico we ascend by three steps to the xystus. Its small extent, not exceeding, in its greatest dimensions, 70 feet by 20, did not permit trees, hardly even shrubs, to be planted in it. The centre, therefore, was occupied by a pavement; and on each side boxes filled with earth were ranged for flowers, while, to make amends for the want of real verdure, the whole wall opposite the portico is painted with trellises and fountains, and birds drinking from them; and above, with leafy copses tenanted by numerous tribes of the winged race.

In one corner is situated a summer triclinium, elegantly decorated, and fitted up with couches and a circular table of marble. Overhead was a trellised roof, which was probably adorned with the vine and other climbing plants. The walls are gaily painted in panel, after the prevailing fashion, and with a whimsical frieze above, which consisted of all kinds of table dainties, but has almost entirely disappeared. In front is a small fountain, or, rather, jet of water. On the whole, this retreat, in the radiance of an Italian summer-noon, must have been peculiarly grateful, and have conduced to "slumber sweet, and sweeter dreams."

In the other corner of the garden is a small furnace, either intended for a bath, or to keep water constantly hot for the use of those who preferred their potations warm.

On the right of the atrium is a venereum, carefully secluded, and consisting of a small court, surrounded by a portico of octagonal columns, a sacrarium dedicated to Diana, two cabinets with glazed windows, a triclinium probably provided with curtains, a kitchen, a water-closet, and a staircase leading to the terrace above the portico. The whole is elegantly decorated with gold-coloured ornament, brilliantly tinted columns, and paintings of Mars, Venus, and Cupid, and of Actæon devoured by his dogs for intruding upon the privacy of Diana. In the adjoining lane four skeletons were found, apparently a female attended by three slaves: beside her lay a round plate of silver, together with several golden rings set with engraved stones, two ear-rings, five gold bracelets, and thirty-two pieces of money. Probably she was the fair lady to whom this portion of the house of Sallust was peculiarly appropriated.

The next mansion of special interest is the

HOUSE OF THE DIOSCURI,

also known as that of the Quæstor, which, from its elegance and size, must unquestionably have belonged to some person of wealth and rank.

It consists of three distinct divisions, or rather of two houses connected by a peristyle. Externally as well as internally it is characterized by the utmost minuteness and finish of ornament. The walls are painted in red panels, and relieved by cornices of stucco. At the entrance doorway is a bas-relief of Mercury running away with a purse. Paintings of the Dioscuri—Castor and Pollux—adorn the sides of the vestibule. The atrium, which measures about 40 feet by 31, is paved with *opus signatum* of a reddish hue, derived from the pounded tiles or pottery of which, added to fragments of marble, it was composed.* Here the walls are coloured red and yellow, and embellished with vivid paintings of arabesques, landscapes, and mythic subjects. An open court, surrounded by a colonnade, which varies from 8 to 10 feet in width, appears to have contained a flower-garden; and on the eastern side a large and deep piscina, or pond, in whose centre stood a column, supporting some kind of Triton or Nymph for the supply of water. The entire area of the court was about 80 palms by 47; and as no building on the south or western sides can ever have existed to shut out the warmth and radiance of the sun, the whole must have constantly worn a bright, cheerful, and stimulating aspect, while the por-

JUPITER AND HIS EAGLE.

* Sir W. Gell, "Pompeiana," ii. 16.

tico afforded shade when shade was considered desirable.

On the eastern side opened the great triclinium, or principal banqueting-room, whose walls were enriched with laminæ of rare marbles. These were probably carried off by the owner, some time after the eruption. The principal paintings found here were,—Perseus and Andromeda; Bacchus and a Faun; Medea contemplating the murder of her two children, Mennerus and Pheres; a Dwarf leading an Ape; Hymen with his torch; and a magnificent picture of Jupiter, the "father of gods and men," enthroned in his curule chair, with the imperial eagle at his side.

A third court, or peristyle, enriched by twelve Doric columns, painted red and white, and supporting a rich entablature, contained a compluvium and fountain,—the latter issuing from a species of flower in marble, on which frogs and lizards are seen disporting. The walls of this splendid apartment glowed with fanciful designs in the most vivid colours.

In the *ala*, or wing, attached to this third peristyle, were discovered two very large and richly ornamented wooden chests, lined inside with brass, bound with iron, and provided with handles and locks of bronze. It would appear that the survivors of the fatal eruption had endeavoured to carry off the treasure which these enclosed, and probably succeeded, except where a few coins slipped between the bottom bars. This, indeed, would have been no protection to the coins, had not the excavators fallen into a trifling error, and in working from above, descended into a chamber *behind* the chests; so

COURT OF THE PISCINA OF THE HOUSE OF THE QUÆSTOR.

that it became necessary for them to exhaust the money from these receptacles through a hole perforated in the partition-wall.

The adjoining cubicula, or *ædes domesticæ*—their uses are uncertain—contain various pictures. In one is a sketch of Cupid and a youth sitting by the edge of a stream; a Bacchante; a dancing-girl carrying a garland; and Diana descending from the skies to woo Endymion.

These are the principal curiosities discovered in the House of the Quæstor. Adjoining it stands the

HOUSE OF THE CENTAUR,

also called the House of Apollo, and the House of Meleager and Atalanta, whose principal features are a Corinthian atrium; a triclinium opening on a garden; the venereum; some subterranean cellars; and numerous fine mosaics and paintings—notably one of Meleager and Atalanta—which are now preserved in the Neapolitan Museum.

I shall now glance very briefly, for my limits will not admit of detailed description, at those other houses in Pompeii which have been distinguished by particular appellations, and which present some point of interest. For fuller information I may refer my readers to the elaborate work of Overbeck.

In the STREET OF HERCULANEUM :—

The *Inn of Albinus*, also, from an inscription on the walls, named of Julius Polybius, should be noticed. Here, on the door-posts, we see those time-honoured *chequers* which figure on the sign of so many English inns. From their colour—red—and their similarity to a lattice, they were corruptly called the Red Lattice, a word frequently used by early English writers to signify an alehouse. Thus, the dramatist Marston says, "As well known by my wit, as an ale-house by a red lattice;" and in an old ballad (1656) we read :—

> " The tap-house fits them for a jail,
> The jail to the gibbet sends them without fail;
> For those that through a *lattice* sang of late,
> You oft find *crying* through an iron *grate*."*

* Brand, "Popular Antiquities," ii. 353.

The chequers probably indicated that some game was played in the tavern, or hostelry, resembling our modern "draughts."

House of the Vestals.*—This is a double house, with an atrium, a triclinium, and other apartments, once richly decorated with paintings and mosaics, but now very bare and desolate. In a room called the *lararium*, with three recesses, stands an altar, whereon the sacred fire is supposed to have been cherished by the Vestal Virgins.†

House of the Chirurgeon.—The forty surgical instruments found here have been removed to the Museum at Naples.

The *Ponderarium, Custom,* or *Weighing-House.*—Numerous balances and weights were discovered in this building; one with the inscription, " C Pon Tal" (100 talents); others lettered "*Eme et Habetis*" (Buy and thou shalt have).

Soap Factory.—This contained the usual materials and implements for soap-making.

Tavern of Phœbus.—Here were found the skeletons of a man and two horses, with an inscription purporting that " Phœbus and his customers request the patronage of M. Holconius Priscus and C. Gaulus Rufus, the Duumvirs."

Public Bakehouse, with the usual adjuncts.

Blacksmith's Shop.

House of Julius Polybius, with three stories.

---

* So named by Sir W. Gell.

† "In this secret and sacred place the most solemn and memorable days of the family were spent in rejoicing; and here, on birth-days, sacrifices were offered to Juno, or the Genius, as the protector of the new-born chiid."—*Bonucci.*

STREET OF NARCISSUS :—

This contains the *House of the Dancing Girls;* so named from a picture of four Bacchanals.

House of Narcissus, or *House of Apollo.*—Called the former, from an elegant picture of Narcissus; and the latter, from a bronze statue of the god. Numerous surgical instruments have been discovered here.

STREET OF MODESTUS :—

House of the Painted Columns; House of Neptune; House of Flowers; House of Modestus, so named from an inscription in red on the walls of the opposite house; *House of Pansa* (see p. 212).

STREET OF LA FULLONICA :—

House of Apollo, excavated in 1838.—Here were found two fine mosaics, representing the quarrel between Achilles and Agamemnon, and Achilles at the Court of Lycomedes; several admirably-executed bronzes; exquisitely-designed paintings of Apollo, Juno, and Venus; and other eloquent evidences of the wealth and taste of the former owner.

House of Adonis, excavated in 1836; so named from a fresco of Adonis, when wounded by the wild boar, receiving the consolations of Venus. The " pictured walls" also set forth the fable of Hermaphroditus and the nymph Salmacis.

Houses of the Fountains, the Fullonica, House of the Tragic Poet.—Already described (pp. 190-209).

STREET OF THE MERCURIES :—
House of Inachus and Io. ·

ACHILLES AT THE COURT OF LYCOMEDES.

House of the Nereids, also called *House of Meleager*. The front is faced with a plain white stucco, resting on a plinth coloured in imitation of gray marble. The walls of the vestibule exhibit three broad bands of colour: the lower, black; the centre, red; the upper, white. The black is ornamented with caryatides, bearing javelins, which suspend rich festoons of fruit and flowers; the red, with bright arabesques of an architectural character, intermingled with Bacchantes; and the white, with other groups of caryatides, architectural ornament, and priestesses. Very beautiful and fantastic is the general appearance of the atrium, with its marble fountain, marble baths, mosaic pavement, and painted walls. A dark-red plinth surrounds the room, and represents lively Nereids disporting with grim sea-lions and other ocean - monsters; and the pictures embody several of those fables with which Ovid has made every schoolboy familiar: Vulcan forging armour for Æneas, Paris and Helen, Dædalus and Pasiphae.*

ALLEGORICAL FIGURE.

It is a chamber for a poet, where he might endlessly "chew the cud" of pleasant fancies.

If the poet were content with the atrium, show me

* "Pompeii" (Library of Entertaining Knowledge), ii 261, 262.

the artist that would not be well pleased with the peristyle, one of the most magnificent and most capacious apartments in Pompeii. The portico consists of twenty-four columns, whose upper portion is painted white, the lower red. The impluvium, which once bloomed with flowering plants and evergreens, is surrounded by a channel of stone, to conduct the rain-water into the reservoir. A graceful reservoir, let me tell you! For it is edged with a marble coping, and its stucco lining is painted of an intensely vivid azure. It was anciently fed with a double supply: from a central column, and from a fountain at the further end, which poured its waters in a miniature cascade down a flight of eight little steps. A square basin, communicating with the reservoir, probably served for a fish-pond, where Lalage or Nicera might feed her gold and silver fish. The walls are alive, so to speak, with frolicsome Nereids—surely the owner was captain of some "stately argosy!"—and of their numerous paintings, seventeen still retain much of their original freshness.

From the peristyle the stranger passes into another large apartment—a room without a name. It contains two tiers of columns, one above the other; the upper surrounded by a gallery, something like the arcade and clerestory of a Gothic church. The capitals of these columns are heavily ornamented in a semi-Corinthian style. Walls, columns, and pictures are all monochrome—that is, painted in one colour, the colour being yellow, perhaps to imitate gold. The only subjects now discernible are, Theseus rescuing Ariadne from the Minotaur, and Tiresias metamorphosed into a woman.

Adjoining is another large chamber, which seems to have been undergoing repair at the time of the eruption; and beyond this the great triclinium, a room of magnificent dimensions and superb decorations. Over the smaller apartments it is unnecessary to linger; they are not unworthy, however, of this most superb mansion.

House of the Centaur, House of the Dioscuri, already described. There are also to be seen in this street the *House of the Five Skeletons, House of Amymone and Neptune* (or *the Anchor*), and *House of Flora and Zephyrus.*

STREET OF THE FAUN :—

In this street there are but two houses worth notice: the *House of the Labyrinth,* so named from a mosaic pavement of admirable workmanship, which illustrates the old fable of Theseus and the Minotaur; and the *House of the Faun,* which contains a beautiful bronze statuette of a Dancing Faun, and a large mosaic of the Battle of the Granicus. This latter mansion is remarkable for its Egyptian mosaics, nearly all of them bearing especial reference to the worship of Osiris. The furniture and utensils found here were of unusual richness; and the gems, rings, bracelets, necklaces, were scarcely less eloquent witnesses to the wealth and refinement of their owners.

The six streets which we have thus rapidly traversed all run in one direction—namely, from north to south, or from the City Walls to the Street of the Baths.

The Street of the Baths lies north-west and south-east,

cutting through the city in nearly a straight line, from the junction of the Street of Herculaneum to the Gate of Isis, on the Nola Road, and bisected about midway by the Street of Stabiæ. A portion of it is called the Street of Fortune, but for the convenience of the reader we shall adhere to one general appellation—

THE STREET OF THE BATHS.

Here, at the junction of the street with a second Street of Fortune (running towards the Forum), we find the remains of a Triumphal Arch and Fountain. In this vicinity are situated the Temple of Fortune and the older Thermæ (see pp. 97, 154).

Pursuing our route, we may notice the ruins of several shops, one of an ironmonger, and another belonging to a statuary; the *House of the Chase,* so called from one of its paintings; the *House of the Bronze Figures,* where several two-headed busts of Hermes, in bronze, were discovered; the *House of the Black Walls,* in one of whose chambers a variety of graceful ornament is depicted on a black ground; the *House of the Figured Capitals*—those of the pilasters at the entrance doorway being sculptured with Fauns and Bacchantes; the *House of the Grand Duke of Tuscany* (excavated in 1832), where the visitor regards with admiration a fine representation of the old fable of Amphion and Dirce; and the *House of Ariadne,* whose more interesting objects are its pictures of Ariadne, Galatea, and the Love-Merchant—the latter, an old man with a cage of Cupids, one of whom he offers for sale to two young maidens attracted by the novelty of his wares.

In a street called the *Vico Storto*, which branches off on the right, are situated several houses of minor interest. Continuing our route towards the Nola Gate, we pass a series of shops and houses which have been but partially excavated.

We shall now retrace our steps a few hundred yards, and turn into the

STREET OF STABIÆ.

Beginning at the Stabiæ Gate, we see on our right the Odeum, the Great Theatre, and the so-called Barracks; on our left, the House of Iphigenia, so named from a painting discovered in it which represents Orestes and Pylades brought as prisoners into the presence of Agamemnon's daughter. In this direction the excavations of the buried city are, at present, being conducted. A road leading towards the Amphitheatre passes the

Villa of Julia Felix, excavated in 1754-55, but covered up again. An inscription was found here purporting that the owner, Julia Felix, was willing to let for a term of five years, a bath, a venereum, and ninety shops with terraces and upper chambers.

In the Street of Stabiæ we find :

The *House of Lucretius*, or *delle Sonatrici*, excavated in 1867, a mansion remarkable for its dimensions and the elegance of its decorations. Its name has been satisfactorily ascertained from a painting, now in the Naples Museum, which introduced a scroll or letter addressed to " M. Lucretio Flam. Martis Decurioni Pompei (io) "— that is, to Marcus Lucretius, Priest of Mars, and Decurion of Pompeii*—as also a stylus and ink-bottle. The atrium has a pavement of white mosaic. The walls are painted, the lower part in imitation of vari-coloured marbles; the upper in blue, relieved with fanciful ornament. A *lararium*, or shrine of the Lares, stands on the right of the entrance. The tablinum, raised one step above the level of the atrium, is also paved with white marble mosaic, and in the centre with a slab of *giallo antico*. The walls are decorated with architectural designs; the ceiling (of stucco) with panels in colours and gilt rosettes. In the peristyle, which is six or seven feet higher than the tablinum, a curious alcove-fountain is enriched with mosaics, paintings, shell-work, and a small marble image of Silenus. On his left the water issues from a sort of leather bottle, and falls into a square stone channel, which conducts it into a circular basin in the middle of the court. This basin, about seven feet in diameter and two feet in depth, has in its centre a hollow pedestal, which gives room for a *jet-d'eau*. On each side stands a double figure: one representing a Faun and a Bacchante, the other Ariadne and Bacchus. Numerous sculptures are scattered around, and the basin is ornamented with figures of ducks, cows, ibises, and the like, so that the scene may not unjustly be compared to a statuary's yard in the Marylebone Road! But as the house appears to have been undergoing repair at the time of the eruption, it is possible the owner collected his treasures in this particular apartment, as safest from accidental injury.

The articles discovered here included vases, cande-

* Overbeck, "Pompeii"

labra, surgical instruments, glass bottles shaped like animals, bronze coins, theatrical pictures of a tragic and comic character, bronze ornaments, culinary vessels in bronze, and a four-wheeled waggon.

Near what are called the New Thermæ stands a recently-excavated house, that of *Diadumenus*, chiefly remarkable for its portico, its elegant atrium, and handsome lararium.

Immediately in front of the Baths is the *House of C. Cornelius Rufus*, discovered in 1861, containing a spacious and finely decorated atrium, with a central impluvium, and a table of marble supported by lions; a peristyle, surrounded by Doric columns; cubicula, and other apartments, embellished with frescoes of unusual merit; several bronzes, and a well-executed bust of the owner of the house, inscribed with his name.

The recent excavations in this quarter have revealed several interesting houses: one, which seems to have been a species of tavern, is known, from a painting on the outer wall, as the Elephant Inn;* a second, distinguished by its handsome triclinium, contains a noble specimen of the ancient painters—" Hercules, while overcome by wine, is robbed of his arms by Cupids;" the third, a baker's shop, possesses an oven in which eighty-three loaves of bread were found half-baked; and the fourth, a handsome private mansion, is remarkable for its marble fountain and its mythological paintings.

* A sign, or tablet, records that one Sitticio had recently restored the tavern, and offers travellers a triclinium with three beds, and every comfort.

HOSPITVM . HIC . LOCATVR.
TRICLINIVM . CVM. TRIBVS . LECTIS
SIT . COMM . . . (ET COMMODA).

The only streets which now remain to be noticed are those of the Augustals, of the Dii Consentes, and the Street of Abundance.

In the former are situated the *House of Venus and Mars;* the *House of Ganymede;* the *House of the King of Prussia*, excavated in 1822; and the *House of Queen Adelaide*, opened in the presence of the late Queen-Dowager in 1838.

In the Street of the Dii Consentes the visitor's attention is directed to the *House of Hero and Leander*, the *House of Apollo and Coronis*, and the *House of Adonis*, the latter containing some remarkable pictures, especially a caricature sketch of a painter's studio.

Lastly, in the Street of Abundance, we meet with several handsome shops, the remains of two fountains, the *House of the Wild Boar* (so called from a mosaic in the prothyrum), the *House of the Physician* (where seventy surgical instruments and the apparatus for pill-making and ointment-making were discovered), the *House of the Graces*, and the *House of the Emperor Francis II*. None of these require a detailed notice, as the articles of interest which they formerly contained have been removed to the Museum at Naples.

VIEW OF THE VILLA OF DIOMEDES.

IX.

The Tombs at Pompeii.

"There, while the fire lies smouldering on the ground,
My bones, the all of me, can then be found.
Arrayed in mourning robes, the sorrowing pair
Shall gather all around with pious care;
With ruddy wine the relics sprinkle o'er,
And snowy milk on them collected pour.
Then with fair linen cloths the moisture dry,
Inurned in some cold marble tomb to lie.
With them inclose the spices, sweets, and gums,
And all that from the rich Arabia comes,
And what Assyria's wealthy confines send,
And tears, sad offering, to my memory lend."
　　　　　　　　　TIBULLUS, Eleg. iii. 2–17.

HE interment of the dead was celebrated by the Romans with peculiar pomp. It formed, indeed, an important part of their religion, for it was their belief that if the body remained unburied, the soul wandered, forlorn and desolate, through the sorrowful lapse of a hundred years, on the hither side of the Styx, unable to obtain admission to its final resting-place. The survivors, therefore, were necessarily anxious that their deceased kinsmen or friends should receive the homage of decent sepulture. So after the corpse had been duly washed and dressed, and seven days of watching and wailing had passed by, it was borne in solemn procession, attended by a long array

of mourners, musicians, and stage-mimes; by numerous vehicles containing waxen masks of its ancestors, by the slaves whom the will of the departed had emancipated, by a weeping train of the nearest relations, to the appointed place of burial.* This, by the Roman law, was almost invariably without the city, and generally near a public highway. Here, if the family possessed a patrimonial tomb, the dead was laid within it; or else within the sepulchre which, during his life, he would have constructed for the purpose. The poor were interred in public cemeteries, called *puticuli*, from the trenches (*puteis*) ready excavated to receive bodies. In most cases the corpse was burned—for the practice of incremation prevailed among the Romans from the first century before Christ until the establishment of Christianity—at the place of burial, which was then named *bustum* (as if from *buro, uro, comburo,* to burn). The funeral pile (*rogus*) was built of rough wood, unpolished by the axe. Pitch was used to stimulate the flames; and cypress, to overpower with its pungent odours the exhalations from the burning body. As the combustion proceeded, the bystanders cast various offerings into the flames; the robes, arms, treasures, and favourite animals of the deceased; and the precious oils and unguents of the East.

When reduced to ashes, these were quenched with wine, and carefully deposited in an urn of marble, bronze, silver, or terra-cotta. The presiding priest then sprinkled the mourning crowd three times with a branch

---

* See Bekker's "Gallus," for a minute account of the funeral ceremonies of the Romans; also, article *Funus* in Dr. Smith's "Dictionary of Antiquities."

STREET OF TOMBS.

of olive or laurel dipped in water, as a sign of purification, and gave the word, *Ilicet* (*Ire licet*), Depart! And the procession, uttering their last farewell with the cry of *Vale* or *Salve*, returned to their several abodes.

The urn was committed to the tomb on the following day. There were two sorts of tombs; which may roughly be designated *family*, and *private* tombs. To the former the ashes of the freed slaves of the family were frequently admitted. On the ninth day after death, the funeral feasts (*novemdialia*) were celebrated; and the dead were also honoured at intervals with sacrifices (*inferiæ*) offered to their manes. The inferiæ consisted principally of libations of milk, wine, or blood, the smell of which was supposed to be peculiarly acceptable to their ghosts. The tomb was likewise crowned with garlands of flowers—of roses, lilies, myrtle, and the amaranth—a custom which has descended to our own time.

> " Full canisters of fragrant lilies bring,
> Mixed with the purple roses of the spring ;
> Let me with funeral flowers his body strew,—
> This gift, which parents to their children owe,
> This unavailing gift, at least I may bestow."—VIRGIL.

At Pompeii the tombs are situated on either side of the road that leads from the Herculaneum Gate towards the Torre dell' Annunziata, in the Pagus Augustus Felix, an aristocratic suburb of the city. Commencing our progress at what I may term the further end, the first sepulchral monument we meet with is the

Cenotaph of Diomedes, situated opposite the villa which is supposed to have belonged to the same owner. It is a solid building of rubble-work, faced with stucco, and not unlike a small temple in appearance.* It is about nine feet broad and twelve feet high, with a pilaster at either side supporting a pediment. Under the pediment you may read the following inscription :—

M . ARRIVS . ⁞ . L . . DIOMEDES
SIBI . SVIS . MEMORIÆ
MAGISTER . PAG . AUG . FELIX . SVBVRB.

Which is Englished thus :—

<blockquote>Marcus Arrius Diomedes, freedman of Iulia (?), chief magistrate of the suburb Augustus Felix, [erected this building] to the memory of himself and family.</blockquote>

Beneath are sculptured the fasces, the emblems of magisterial authority, but reversed, in conformity with the usages of mourning. On the left is a wall which separates the principal tomb from two funereal cippi with hemispheres, the hinder part of each carved in imitation of the human hair; one erected to Arria, the daughter of Diomedes, and the other to Arrius his son. An inscription under the wall—Arriæ . M . F(iliæ) . Diomedes . L . Sibi . Svis—shows that they belonged to the same family. Close to the platform, in a small semi-circular niche, is the cippus of a child, Velasius Gratus, ætat. 12; and near it moulder in decay the tombs of Salvius, a child of five years old, and of Servilia.

Tomb of Cenis and Labeo: an oblong building, the sides ornamented with pilasters, which formerly supported an entablature, crowned by statues. Of these only the fragments remain. The front exhibits the ruins of two bas-reliefs, which we may suppose to have contained

* Overbeck, " Pompeji," ii. 23.

portraits of the duumvirs, Caius Cenis and Lucius Labeo, to whom the tomb was erected by their freedman Menomachus.

Tomb of the Libellæ.—This is a solid building of blocks of travertin, in form resembling the pedestal of a column; base about twelve feet square, height sixteen feet. It has a moulding and cornice, and the following inscription:—

M . ALLEIO . LVCCIO . LIBELLÆ . PATRI . ÆDILI
II . VIR . PRÆFECTO . QVINQ . ET . M . ALLEIO . LIBELLÆ . F .
DECVRIONI . VIXIT . ANNIS . XVII . LOCVS . MONVMENTI
PVBLICE . DATVS . EST . ALLEIA . M . F . DECIMILLA . SACERDOS .
PVBLICA . CERERIS . FACIENDVM . CVRAVIT.. VIRO . ET . FILIO.

[To M. Alleius Luccius Libella, the father, Ædile, Duumvir,* Quinquennial, and Prefect; and M.˙Alleius Libella, his son, Decurion, who lived seventeen years, was assigned the site of this monument at the public expense. Alleia Decimilla, daughter of Marcus, Public Priestess of Ceres, erected it to her husband and son.]

Cicero in one of his letters informs a friend who had requested his interest in obtaining a decurionship at Pompeii, that it was easier to become a Roman consul than a Pompeian decurion.† The reply may have been partly intended in jest, but yet we must infer that the post of decurion in the gay Campanian city was one of great honour, and hence that the Libellæ, one of whom was a duumvir, and the other a decurion in his seventeenth year, belonged to a wealthy and influential family.

Tomb with the Marble Door (*Colla porta marmorea*).— At the junction of the two roads stands a closed tomb,

---

* The offices of Duumvir and Decurion corresponded to those of the Roman Consul and Senators.—" Pompeii " (Lib. Ent. Knowl.), ii. 26

Overbeck, " Pompeji," ii, 26.

built of small pieces of tufa, laid sometimes horizontally and sometimes diamond-wise (*opus reticulatum*). Its entrance, about four feet high, is closed by a marble door, which turns upon bronze pivots let into sockets of the same metal. The interior consists of a small chamber lighted by a small window in the roof. Around it runs a stone ledge, on which, as well as in certain vaulted niches, were deposited the urns or vases containing the ashes of the dead. There were also several bronze lamps, used, I conjecture, to light up the dark and silent sepulchre, when the kinsmen of the deceased visited it to perform their sacrificial rites (*inferiæ*). A small square enclosure, just beyond this tomb, is supposed to have been an *ustrinum*, or place for burning dead bodies.

Crossing to the other side of the road, we perceive the *Funeral Triclinium* (*Triclinium für die Leichenmahle*), an enclosed area of irregular figure, about twenty feet long, stuccoed, and unadorned except by a low pediment and cornice. Enter,—the doorway is low,—enter, and you find yourself within an unroofed chamber, whose walls are gaily embellished with paintings of birds and flowers. Before you stands a stone triclinium, with a massive pedestal in the centre for a table, and a round pillar immediately in advance of it. Here was celebrated the *silicernium*, or funeral feast, which completed the honours paid to the dead by their survivors, and which an ungrateful or disappointed heir occasionally withheld. On the round column probably stood the urn or vase which contained the ashes of the departed. As no other triclinium has been discovered in Pompeii, it seems probable that this one was built for the general accommodation, and perhaps let out to hire.*

Tomb of Nævoleia Tyche and Munatius Faustus.—A family tomb, consisting of a square building surrounded by a wall. Within the enclosure is a sepulchral chamber, surmounted by a marble cippus, richly ornamented, and raised on two steps. The front is occupied by a bas-relief, and by the following inscription :—

<pre>
NÆVOLEIA . I . LIB . TYCHE . SIBI . ET
C . MVNATIO . FAVSTO . AVG . ET . PAGANO
CVI . DECVRIONES . CONSENSV . POPVLI
BISELLIVM . OB . MERITA . EIVS . DECREVERVNT .
HOC . MONIMENTVM . NÆVOLEIA . TYCHE . LIBERTIS . SVIS .
LIBERTATVSQ . ET . C . MVNATI . FAVSTI . VIVA . FECIT .
</pre>

[Nævoleia Tyche, freedwoman of Julia Tyche, to herself and to Caius Munatius Faustus, Augustal, and chief magistrate of the suburb, to whom the Decurions, with the consent of the people, have granted the bisellium in acknowledgment of his merits. Nævoleia Tyche erected this monument in her lifetime for her freedmen and women, and for those of C. Munatius Faustus.]

The bas-relief exhibits a portrait of Nævoleia, and in the lower portion, a funeral group offering sacrifice, or the dedication of the tomb. On one side are the municipal magistrates, on the other the family of Nævoleia and Faustus, each member carrying a vase or bowl ; in the centre, a low altar, upon which a youth is depositing some sacrificial cake, and by it a low semicircular cippus representing the tomb.

* An inscription on the central pedestal, however, records the erection of the triclinium to Vibrius Saturninus by his freedman Callistus.

Each side of the tomb is enriched with a bas-relief. One of them represents the *bisellium*, or seat of honour in the theatre, appropriated to Munatius by decree of the Decurions; the other, a ship entering port—in allusion either to the pursuits of the said Munatius, or, allegorically, to the safe arrival of the barque of the soul in the tranquil haven of the grave.

The ship itself has a raised deck, a figure-head of Minerva, and a swan's neck at the stern supporting a flag-staff; another flag floats from the mast-head. The mast has a long yard, which carries a square sail; two boys on the yard are furling the sail, while a third who has been rendering assistance aloft descends by a rope, a fourth is climbing the shrouds, and a man on deck clews up the canvas. At the helm sits the master—probably Munatius himself—and directs their movements.

In the interior of the chamber, and on the stone bench surrounding it, several cinerary urns were discovered, as well as some lamps, and three urns of glass, which contained burnt bones saturated in a mixture of water, wine, and oil—the last libation probably made by the survivors. A small niche in the wall of the enclosure contains a cippus, or funeral column, engraved with the name of Caius Munatius Atimetus, who died at the age of fifty-seven.

I think we need not tarry at

The Tomb of the Istacidian Family—a small plot of ground, about fifteen feet square, containing no monuments, but simply three cippi, inscribed to Istacidius Helenus, Istacidius Januarius, and to Istacidia Scapidia and Mesonia Satulla.* But the next erection commands our notice by its architectural pretensions.

Cenotaph of C. Calventius Quietus.—Within a court about twenty-one feet square, rises a podium, or basement, of three steps, on which a square marble altar-monument is placed, adorned with small square pinnacles called *acroteria*. These acroteria are enriched with bas-reliefs, now sadly dilapidated, of Fame and Victory, of Theseus, of Œdipus solving the riddle of the Sphinx, and of the Funeral Pile, on which the remains of Quietus were consumed. The cenotaph is further adorned with richly-carved garlands of oak-leaves, bound with fillets ; the cornice and mouldings merit praise both for design and execution. From the sculpture of a bisellium, or seat of honour, on the front, we know that the sepulchre before us is that of an Augustal, and our inference is confirmed by the inscription above it :—

C . CALVENTIO . QVIETO
AVGVSTALI
HVIC . OB . MVNIFICENT . DECVRIONVM
DECRETO . ET . POPVLI . CONSENSV . BISELLII .
HONOR DATVS . EST .

[To Caius Calventius Quietus, Augustal. To him, on account of his public spirit, the honour of the Bisellium was decreed by the Decurions, with the consent of the people.]

An empty space intervenes between this and the next tomb—the so-called *Round Tomb;* consisting of a short circular tower on a square basis, and surrounded by a wall, which is adorned with acroteria, and the acroteria

* Overbeck, " Pompeji.

with bas-reliefs. One of these represents a female with a patera and garland in her hand in the act of offering some fruits upon an altar; another, a young mother in a flowing Greek robe depositing a funereal fillet on her dead child. As its skeleton seems to rest on a pile of stones, Mazois conjectures that the child perished in the earthquake.* The sepulchral chamber contains three niches with sepulchral vases, two of which were empty when discovered; and the walls and vaulted roof are enriched with arabesques, swans, and peacocks.

Tomb of Patricius Scaurus: so called from an inscription found in the vicinity, but which Overbeck does not consider to have belonged to the tomb. This is a stately monument—a square cippus of brick resting on three steps, which are raised upon a square basement serving as a sepulchral chamber. The basement and the steps were formerly ornamented with bas-reliefs of gladatorial subjects, which have been already described (see pp. 114, 115).

Tomb of Tyche: a sepulchral enclosure with a cippus, belonging, as an inscription records, to Tyche, *Venerea* of Julia, daughter of Augustus. Beneath it is a columbarium, with fourteen niches.

Passing by the so-called Suburban Inn—the *Tomb of the Glass Amphora* (*Tomba del Vaso di vetro blu*), a square basement-chamber, in which was found a singularly graceful amphora of blue glass with white figures in relief—the Villa of Cicero, remarkable for its fine paint-

* Mazois, " Les Ruines de Pompeii," p. 46.

ings and mosaics, now preserved in the Museum at Naples,
—we come to

The *Hemicycle*, a species of semicircular vaulted alcove, flanked with pilasters, surmounted by a pediment, and painted in red panels with golden arabesques, which seems to have been intended as a resting-place for the weary wayfarer. Near this spot were discovered the skeletons of a mother and her three children, one of them an infant, all interlaced in each other's arms. They had attempted to escape; their strength failed them, or the horrors of the scene paralysed their energies; and they contentedly laid down to die, folded in one last embrace of love stronger than death. From the gold rings and rich ornaments found about them, they must have belonged to a family of distinction.

Tomb of the Garlands, supported on a lofty basement, with Corinthian pilasters, which sustain well-executed wreaths of flowers; and the

Cenotaph of Terentius Felix, demand no special notice.

We now arrive at two open *Exedra* or *Hemicycles*. The first is raised on a high step; it is about seventeen feet in diameter, and bears the following inscription, occupying the whole space above the stone seat, which is finished off at each end by a lion's paw :—

    MAMIÆ . P . F . SACERDOTI . PVBLICÆ . LOCVS .
    SEPVLTVR . DATVS . DECVRIONVM . DECRETO .
    [To Mamia, daughter of Porcius, public priestess, a place of burial is assigned by decree of the Decurions.]

At the foot of the hemicycle, an inscription on an

STREET AT POMPEII RECENTLY EXPLORED.

upright stone records that the decurions had granted to M. Porcius a plot of ground twenty-five feet square—probably the burial-place above mentioned—and close adjoining stands the supposed *Tomb of the Priestess Mamia;* a square pile of masonry covered with stucco, and ornamented in front with four Corinthian columns. In the interior, which was painted, and set round with eleven niches, were found some indifferent marble statues, and a pedestal for the support of the funeral urn.

The second hemicycle belonged, as an inscription recorded, to Aulus Veius, a duumvir of justice and a military tribune, to whom the ground had been presented by the decurions and citizens of Pompeii.

Here we complete our survey of the Strada delle Tombe, or Street of Tombs; an appropriate spot for taking leave—as we now must do—of the

CITY OF THE DEAD.

X.

Herculaneum.

<blockquote>
"The miner plods
With torch and mattock ; and, discoursing, shows
The hoarded fragments of Heraclea's woes."
BEATTIE.
</blockquote>

THE discovery of the actual site of Herculaneum was made in 1709, when the Prince d'Elboeuf of Lorraine was erecting a summer-palace at Portici, which he desired to decorate with antiques. Hearing that a peasant at Resina, while sinking a well, had lighted upon some choice relics, he purchased the right of making further excavations. In these he was so far successful that he had obtained numerous statues and some remains of ancient sculpture, when Count Daun, the Austrian viceroy at Naples, interfered, and reclaimed the right of exploration for the Government. Very little, however, has been done underground. The researches made have not led to such interesting results as at Pompeii. The inhabitants, with very few exceptions, appear to have effected their escape, and to have carried with them almost all their movable property. Nor is it an easy matter to conduct any further investigations. Two towns are built upon the strata which successive eruptions of Vesuvius have deposited over the buried city, and its buildings are filled with a coarse kind of tufa, which offers almost insuperable obstacles to the workman. As fast, therefore, as one portion has been excavated, it has been filled up again with the materials removed from another portion, and which it was impossible to carry to the surface. And, moreover, to provide for the security of the houses in the two modern towns—Resina and Portici—it has been found necessary to build up the ruins immediately they have been despoiled of their treasures.

The principal discoveries made at Herculaneum may be briefly enumerated. A temple; a wide street, paved with lava, and lined with porticoes, leading to a second temple; a basilica, erected by Marcus Nonius, the proconsul, measuring 228 feet in length by 132 feet in breadth, and enclosed within a portico of forty-two columns; several blocks of buildings; a large and handsome villa, embellished with fountains, termini, busts, and statues (now in the Museo Borbonico); some Roman tombs; a suburban villa; and the theatre. The latter is the only object now visible underground, and it is so crowded with pillars erected to support the rock above it, that no perfect *coup d'œil* of its arrangements can be anywhere obtained. It is computed to have possessed accommodation for 10,000 spectators. The area consists of nineteen rows of seats, about a foot high by three and a-half feet wide, laid out, like those of the Pompeian theatres, in cunic or wedge-shaped compartments. The volcanic matter at the back of the stage still exhibits the cast of the mask of a human face, almost as distinct as if it had been taken in plaster.

Two inscriptions were found over the architraves of the side entrances to the orchestra. From one of these it appears that the theatre was erected at the cost of Lucius Annius Mammianus Rufus, Censor and Duumvir of Justice; from the other, that the architect was one Numisius, the son of Publius. In a passage behind the postscenium is the well—opening, above ground, in the Cortile S. Giacomo, in the main street of Resina—which was the original cause of the excavations that led to the discovery of the city.

At the right end of the proscenium is a rectangular basement for a statue, which bears the following inscription:—"Ap . Claudio . C . F . Pulchro . Cos . Imp . Herculanenses . Post . Mort." At the left end a similar base is lettered:—"M . Nonio Balbo Præt . et Procons."

The roof and upper story of the building were supported by large square pilasters of red brick, with marble cornices, and the surface was decorated with marble tablets and paintings, many of which have been removed to the Naples Museum. Bronze statues were found here of Drusus and Antonia, and the Muses.

Herculaneum, the reader will remember, was not destroyed, like Pompeii, by showers of ashes, but by a torrent of volcanic mud, which rolled over the city with resistless force, and filling all its edifices nearly to the roof, hardened as it dried into a coarse tufa. It has, therefore, to be cut away by the axe, like solid stone. And for this reason we need not hope that any important discoveries will be made if the Italian Government should resume the excavations.

We bid farewell to the deserted city in the words of a graceful writer, who acknowledges that it is difficult to exaggerate the impression produced on the mind by the ruins of Herculaneum, or the more extensive and interesting remains of the once bright and luxurious Pompeii. " Here," says Miss Kavanagh, " the Past is Present, and rises before us in its meanest details, and therefore in its greatest power. We cannot walk ten steps without feeling, Is it true? Are the people of this city really dead? Are the owners of these shops and houses really gone for ever? Will the worshippers never come back to the temple? Will the citizens never again throng the forum? Is the garden really forsaken for ever? Will children, girls, and slaves never again gather beneath the colonnade of the villa, or look from the terrace at the purple mountains, with their green slopes and the smoke of distant waterfalls? Which is the truest—that Past which surrounds us, and seems so near; or that Present, which fades away from thought, and seems so far when we enter the charmed city?"

And thus, though it be, as Sir Walter Scott emphatically termed it, a City of the Dead, yet shall it also and ever remain for the cultivated mind, for the vivid imagination, a City of the Living. Recall the past; people the noisy theatre and the busy forum; crowd the temple with adoring worshippers; place the beauty in her boudoir and the artist in his studio, the judge on his bench and the soldier at his post; pour through the streets the rushing, animated, restless life of antiquity; and then shall Pompeii and Herculaneum live again, if only in a summer dream.

XI.

Recent Discoveries.

THE excavations still in vigorous prosecution at Pompeii are constantly revealing new treasures and fresh objects of interest. Among these I may refer to a beautiful statuette in bronze, supposed to represent "Narcissus listening to Echo," which has not unjustly been described as the most precious work of the class hitherto obtained from the ruins, and "a masterpiece of ancient art." It was dug out of what appears to have been a washing or scouring establishment, judging from the numerous leaden vats and deep basins of terra-cotta found on the ground floor. You see in it a graceful, rounded, voluptuous figure, naked except for the goat-skin flung loosely over the left shoulder, and the hunter's cothurn or buskins, laced round the ankle, and reaching to the calf of the leg. The head is inclined over the left shoulder, in the act of listening, and the face wears an intent and peculiarly earnest expression. A branch of ivy and ivy-berries is wound among the hair. The right hand is lifted, and the first finger directed to the spot from whence proceeds the voice of the amorous Echo. The left hand rests daintily on the hip. The sockets of the eyes, which had once been filled with silver or ivory, are now empty.

This exquisite statuette would seem to be of Greek workmanship, and the copy, in all probability, of some famous statue. Its execution is admirable; the chiseling clear and vigorous. The forms are softly rounded, and the principles of anatomy conscientiously studied. The discovery of so precious a work of art is in itself an almost sufficient reward for the labour bestowed upon the Pompeian excavations.

An amber figure of Cupid disguising himself in a wig was discovered about 1864. It seems to have been considered an article of great· value, for it had been carried away, with a small collection of silver coins, by some fugitive from the eruption, whose skeleton was found hard by. A lamp of solid gold, weighing thirty-three and a-half ounces, has also been dug up.

Early in 1867 the excavators came upon a hermetically-sealed bronze vessel, which, when opened, was found to contain a considerable quantity of water. Some adventurous bystanders drank of the liquid, and agreed in pronouncing it fresh, clear, and of remarkable softness. It had been preserved for nearly eighteen hundred years.

The works of art and various objects of interest obtained at Pompeii and Herculaneum are preserved in the Museum at Naples. The recent acquisition of the Blaças collection by the British Museum will, however, place within reach of the Londoner seven ancient relics of great value. These are mural paintings, and their beauty and importance are undeniable. From *Pompeii* come the following :—A spirited group of three figures, one of whom is playing the lyre ; a fine representation of Ulysses escaping the blandishments of the Sirens— winged, bird-footed creatures these, with lutes and double pipes, chanting melodiously their weird strains, while sitting on skeleton-strewn rocks which hem in on either side the strait through whose waters the subtle Odysseus guides his barque ; and a temple, or some other stately pillared building ;—knowledge of perspective being clearly shown in the vanishing lines of the architecture and in the water-surface. From *Herculaneum :* Ariadne reclining on the shore, and as she wakes from her slumber, raising her hand in entreaty towards Theseus, who nevertheless urges his rowers to bear his galley with increased speed from the despairing maiden. From *Stabiæ :* Two poets, crowned, and apparently reciting their verses ; a recumbent female figure, holding a vase of flowers in her left hand ; and, lastly, a bird, painted with wonderful truth and finish.

The processes of the excavation are described by a periodical essayist with much liveliness ; and in our brief account we shall freely borrow from his pages.*

We will suppose that the reader is desirous of witnessing a "*scavo.*" Several chambers are generally kept in readiness for this purpose. It has been ascertained from experience that articles of importance are usually found on the ground floor, in the *lapillo* or ashes. The "scavo" is consequently prepared by removing all the volcanic material which covers the building to within about four or five feet of the floor. The entrances to the chamber

---

* "Quarterly Review," No. ccxxx., pp. 335-337.

are then carefully closed with stones, and no one is allowed to go in until the final excavation takes place.

On the appointed day Signor Fiorelli, the director of the works, accompanies the visitor to Pompeii. Twelve or fourteen workmen, under a superintendent, who watches them closely to prevent any petty pilfering, are ready for the day's task. They usually include a couple of skilful excavators, who have to remove, with peculiar caution, the deposit of loose pumice-stones or indurated mud which preserves the antiquities searched for. The remainder of the party consists of women, girls, and boys, who are employed in removing the rubbish. The mode of procedure adopted is scarcely less rude and primitive than that which Mr. Layard pursued at Nineveh. The diggers loosen the earth, which, shovelled into baskets, is carried away by the laughing, singing, jesting Neapolitans to carts ready to receive it. The superintendent, whose well-practised eye detects the smallest object, occasionally picks up a coin or a fragment of metal. Suddenly the excavators stop, and call the director's attention to a discovery. "The colour of the 'lapillo' tells us if an object in bronze or iron is about to be uncovered. If of copper or bronze, the blue oxidation peculiar to Pompeii tints the soil; if of iron, the secret is betrayed by the reddish-brown hue which marks the presence of that metal." An experienced workman, with a kind of trowel, now removes the "lapillo," and by dexterous manipulation contrives to uncover the object of which he is in quest without injuring it; an elegant bronze vase; perhaps—a glass amphora—a cameo or necklace—a statuette—or an iron utensil of extreme rarity. If the thing discovered is of bronze, lead, or glass, it is generally in excellent condition ; if of iron, so much decomposed, as in most cases to fall in pieces on exposure to the air. The object is carefully removed by the superintendent, placed on a tray, and a note made of the place and position in which it was found, and of any peculiar circumstances attending its discovery. A more detailed description is afterwards taken in the receiving-room, and the article finally transferred to the Royal Museum at Naples, or added to the small collection now being formed at Pompeii.

The diggers and carriers resume their labours, and at length the chamber is entirely cleared. We then recognize it to be the "*tablinum*" in the house of a wealthy citizen. The walls are elaborately painted in vivid colours and with fantastic designs. If they are found to be insecure they are immediately strengthened by iron brackets, by wooden props, or buttresses of masonry. The frescoes of superior merit are carefully removed by detaching the plaster from the wall, and over those which are suffered to remain a varnish is spread to protect them from the atmosphere. The pavement is either in simple patterns of black and white tesseræ or of graceful mosaic, adorned with flowers, fruit, masks, or figures in bright colours. "On removing from it the last layer of rubbish we come upon a perfect skeleton. It is that of a woman, probably the mistress of the house. She had attempted to fly on that fatal night, and had thought to save her jewel-case—the '*mundus muliebris*,' 'the woman's all'— inclosed in its wooden casket or pyxis. We find the hinges, the lock, and the ornamental fittings, which, being of bronze and ivory, have been preserved, whilst the wood-work has perished. Scattered around her are its contents—her golden ear-rings; bracelets; and a necklace hung with curious amulets, such as objects in coral, supposed to bring fecundity, a closed hand, with the two fingers extended to ward off the evil eye, a bee in onyx of exquisite workmanship, as an augury of good, and little bells, whose sound drives away contagion; her jewelled rings; a fragment of her ivory comb; her bronze looking-glass; the ivory pins that gathered up her tresses; and a few small glass and alabaster vases and bottles which held her ointments and perfumes. If the lava-mud has penetrated into her chamber, the mould of the casket itself may be preserved, so that a perfect cast may be taken of it; and even the impression of the linen garments which formed part of her wardrobe may be plainly seen. Near her lies a terra-cotta lamp, with its elegant dolphin-shaped cover. It had fallen from her hands when she sunk exhausted, after in vain groping her way through the thick darkness."

The excavations at present are carried on in a part of the town which seems to have been mainly occupied by the lower classes, and consists of shops and houses of a mean character.

One interesting discovery made here is that of a Pompeian Eating-House. On a white marble slab in the front room stood an earthen pipkin, containing small fish, which had apparently been cooked in oil with raisins and onions, and were ready to be served up, when the sudden doom fell upon the town. Into a kind of brick range were let deep basins of earthenware and metal, and beneath them small open fire-places kept warm the various messes. Upon the top were lying the ladles employed in distributing them. A rude tripod of iron upon the earthen floor supported an iron caldron for boiling water, and in the centre of the room was a portable iron cooking stove, of exceedingly ingenious construction. Against the walls were ranged a number of deep bronze trays of various sizes, fitting into one another. A few glass wine-jars were scattered about, and one or two square panes of window-glass.

The inner shop or room contained several earthen amphoræ of various sizes, which had been used for "bottling" select wines. One was lettered, "Frvt T. Clavd. iiii. L. Vitellio. iii. Cos;" from whence we infer that the wine was bottled in the fourth year of the consulate of Tiberius Claudius, and the third of Lucius Vitellius, or A.D. 47. One wine, from the island of Cos, is called "Covm. Granatvm."—the epithet "granatvm" describing, I suppose, some peculiar flavour. It was bought from the cellar of Aierius Felix at Rome—a wine-merchant of repute, perhaps, for the quality of his wares. Another jar is inscribed "Kor. Opt."—*i.e.*, the very best Corcyra. We also meet with a wine called "Old Luna," which appears to have been purchased by a certain Cornelia of M. Valerius Abinnericus, and to have been four years in bottle.

LVN. VET.
A IIII R
X IṁI S
M. VALERI. ABINNERICI.

CORNELIA

The letter R stands, it may be, for Rubrum, "red;" and

X IIII S may refer to the price paid, or the quantity purchased.

At the bottom of this inner room was a baking-oven, whose mouth was still closed with an iron plate, and within which were found eighty-three loaves, black and charred, but still retaining their shape, that of a modern double loaf scored on the top. On the floor lay the iron shovel which was used to remove the loaves from the oven. Various vessels in metal, some bronze trays, and olives, beans, nuts, and onions, were scattered about the room. The workman had been surprised at his work, and just as he left it the stranger gazes upon it, after the lapse of nearly eighteen centuries.

The ruins of Pompeii are now entered at two points, by the Street of the Tombs, and by the gate leading to the Forum. Every visitor pays a fee of two francs, and, in return, is furnished with a plan of the excavations and a guide. It should be noted that the appellations of the houses and streets are being changed. When possible, the name of the owner is substituted, or else his occupation is designated, and the house numbered. In the preceding pages, however, I have thought it advisable to preserve the old and better-known nomenclature.

A museum of Pompeian relics has been established, and a library is in course of formation exclusively devoted to works on Pompeii, or authorities on the arts and sciences of antiquity.

During the winter a corps of five hundred men, women, and children labour at the excavations; in the summer, on account of the unhealthiness of the site, only fifty are employed. It is calculated that the whole city will have been bared to the curiosity of the modern *virtuoso* in another ten years.

As far as we can now judge, says a writer already referred to, Pompeii must have closely resembled in its principal features a modern Eastern city. It is certain that almost every house was provided with a *mænianum* —that is, a projecting gallery or balcony, either open or roofed, which overhung the street, was built of brick, and supported by strong wooden beams or props. The exterior of the houses, however, afforded but little promise of the beauty, grace, and richness within. The sudden change from the naked brick walls facing the narrow street to the spacious peristyle, embellished with paintings, marbles, and coloured frescoes—decorated with flower-beds, made musical with murmuring fountains —and encircled by alcoves and colonnades, into which the ardent rays of an Italian sun were denied entrance by rich tapestries and embroidered hangings, will remind the Oriental traveller of Damascus and Ispahan. Eminently suggestive of an Eastern town, moreover, are the overhanging galleries, with their small latticed windows; the low, small, and even squalid shops, where trade seems to struggle for breathing-space; the marble slabs on which the vendor exposed his wares, and received their price; and the awnings stretched across the street.

I close these references to recent excavations with a striking incident which forcibly recalls to one's mind the terrible "last scene" in the Pompeian drama. And I give it as sketched by M. Marc Monnier with remarkable fidelity and spirit.*

* Marc Monnier, "Pompéi et les Pompéiens" ("Tour du Monde," 1864), 415, 416.

In 1863, he says, under a mass of ruin, the excavators discovered an empty space, at whose bottom some bones were discernible. They immediately summoned M. Fiorelli to the spot, who conceived a felicitous idea. He caused some plaster to be poured while liquid into the hole, and the same operation was renewed at other points where similar bones were thought to be visible. Afterwards the crust of pumice-stone and hard ashes which enveloped, as in a shroud, these objects, having been carefully removed, before the eye were revealed the skeletons of four human corpses. You may see them now in the Museum at Naples.

One of these bodies is that of a woman, near whom ninety-one pieces of money, two silver vases, some keys, and jewels were discovered. She was making her escape with these treasures when overtaken by death in the narrow street. You may see her still, stretched upon her left side; you may distinguish her head-dress, the texture of her clothes, two rings of silver which she wears on her finger; one of her hands is broken—observe the cellular structure of the bone; the left arm is raised and crooked, the delicate hand is clenched, so that the nails, you can see, have entered the flesh; all the body appears swollen and contracted; the legs alone, very slender, remain extended; you perceive that she struggled in a prolonged agony; her attitude is that of suffering, not of death.

Behind her have fallen a woman and a young girl; the elder—her mother, perhaps—was of humble birth, to judge from the size of her ears; she wore on her finger only a ring of iron; her left leg raised and stretched,

BODIES DISCOVERED AMONG THE RUINS OF POMPEII.

shows that she too has suffered, though less than the noble lady; the poor lose less in dying! Near her, as if on the same bed, lies her young daughter; one is at the head, the other at the foot; their legs cross. This young girl, almost a child, produces a strange impression on the spectator; you can clearly discern the texture, the folds of her clothing—the linen which covered her arm down to the wrist—some rents here and there exposing the skin—and the embroidery of the small shoes which encased her feet; above all, you see her last hour, her supreme moment, as if one had been present at it, under the wrath of Vesuvius—she had raised her robe over her head in her terror; she fell, while running, with her face

BODY DISCOVERED AMONG THE RUINS OF POMPEII.

against the ground, and being unable to rise, had supported on one arm her young and feeble head. One hand is open, as if she had held something—perhaps the veil which covered her. The finger-bones pierce through the plaster; she did not endure any long pain, yet upon her it is most pitiful to look; she was not fifteen years old.

The fourth body is that of a man of gigantic stature. He has flung himself on his back to die bravely; his arms and legs are straight, and immovable. His clothes are very sharply defined, the tunic which once was new and brilliant, the sandals (soleæ) laced to the feet, with the iron nails that fastened the wooden soles still plainly discernible. On the bone of one finger he wears a ring of iron; his mouth is open, and some teeth are wanting; his nose and cheek-bones are boldly marked; the eyes and hair have disappeared, but the moustache remains. There is a martial and resolute air in this fine corpse.

Such, then, are the scenes which occasionally meet one's gaze in the excavations at Pompeii.

XII.
The Museum at Naples.

MUZEO NATIONALE—TREASURES FROM POMPEII.

S I have already stated, the principal discoveries made at Pompeii and Herculaneum are preserved in the National Museum of Naples (formerly called the Muzeo Borbonico), and my view of the treasures of antiquity which their excavation has revealed can hardly be considered complete without brief reference to them. It is true that a mere enumeration of these choice and precious things can be of no interest to the reader, while my space precludes me from enlarging on their value as illustrations of ancient art, manners, and customs. Yet am I unwilling to quit the subject without affording some idea of their extent and character.

First, as to the *Frescoes*.

Overbeck is of opinion that the Pompeians employed three distinct kinds of mural painting.* Pure fresco; fresco in which the colours are laid on thickly in the centre, but diminish towards the edges; and a kind of

---

* Overbeck, "Pompeji," ii. 174–219. An elaborate examination of the fresco work of the ancients will be found in the pages here referred to.

tempera, or painting on dry stucco, in which the body of colour is thin, but laid on evenly throughout. Pure fresco paintings are rare, but the walls were almost invariably prepared in this way as grounds for designs executed in one of the other two methods. The general style of execution is free, bold, and vigorous; the artists were evidently Greeks, or brought up in a Greek school; and their work is almost wholly of a decorative character. It must therefore be judged from this point of view; not as the compositions of a great master, carefully matured, and designed for an independent existence, but as the swift and spirited productions of a ready "brush," intended to embellish the walls of an atrium or a tablinum. The subjects are selected with a fine eye to effect; the colouring is always vivid and impressive; the ornamentation shows an exhaustible wealth of fancy; and one cannot help wishing that our English mansions were similarly brightened and enriched by things of equal beauty.

Most noticeable in the Muzeo Nationale are the following frescoes, some of which have been described in the preceding pages:—

The Love-Merchant offering for sale a cage full of Cupids. A handsome lady leans against a pillar, while the merchant pulls from his cage a little Cupid by the wing. Two more remain in it; two have previously been released; while a fifth, who best succeeds in engaging the lady's attention, flies towards her with two garlands in his hands.

The Sacrifice of Iphigenia, supposed to be a copy of the celebrated picture by Timanthes, which Pliny has described (Hist. Nat., xxxv. 10, s. 36).

SOME NOTABLE SPECIMENS. 271

Ariadne deserted by Theseus.

Achilles instructed by Chiron to play upon the lyre. The contrast of colours is particularly well managed and striking.

ACHILLES INSTRUCTED BY CHIRON TO PLAY UPON THE LYRE.

Pylades and Orestes, chained, and led away to the sacrifice.

Achilles delivering Briseis to the heralds of Agamemnon—a *chef-d'œuvre* of ancient art.

Theseus slaying the Minotaur.

Telephus nourished by the Hind, while Hercules, Pan, and Fortune attend him—this was removed from Herculaneum.

Antiope's revenge: Circe bound to the horns of the bull.

Medea contemplating the death of her children, who, meanwhile, are amusing themselves at play—a nobly conceived and admirably executed composition, imitated, it is supposed, from the famous picture by Timomachus of Byzantium, with which Julius Cæsar enriched his temple to Venus Genitrix.

The marriage of Bacchus and Ariadne—full of "poetical intention."

Masinissa and Sophonisba—an historical picture. Sophonisba holds the "poisoned cup," which Masinissa, while embracing her, prevails upon her to drink, that she may escape the ignominy of figuring in Scipio's triumph.

The Seven Days of the Week, represented by the seven planets.

The Danzatrice, or Dancing-Girls.

Mars and Venus.

We now pass to the *Mosaics*, which at Pompeii were employed not only for pavements but for mural decoration. The "Battle of Issus" is the largest and finest ancient mosaic now extant. It was found in the House of the Faun; as were Acrates riding on a tiger, or panther; and a decorative design of masks and wreaths.

I have referred, in a preceding section, to the *choragium*, or rehearsal, which exhibits the choragus instructing the performers in their parts. Equally noteworthy are :—

Lycurgus attacked by Bacchantes and a panther for ordering the vines to be destroyed.

Theseus conquering the Minotaur.

The Three Graces.

A magpie stealing a mirror out of a basket.

Sculptures.—The priestess Eumachia; the statue erected in her honour by the guild of *fullones*, or dyers, at Pompeii.

And from Herculaneum :—Hercules and Omphale; a fine Roman bust of Alexander the Great, wearing the two small horns, insignia of divinity, as son of Jupiter Ammon; a colossal figure of Claudius, seated; a colossal seated statue of Jupiter, with the head of Augustus; the fine statue known as Aristides, though by some critics called Æschines—a masterpiece of high intellectual expression, the embodiment in marble of the tranquil dignity of Genius; the Muses, found in the theatre at Herculaneum; busts of Bacchus, Demosthenes, and Themistocles; and statues of Cicero, Homer, and Sulla.

Bronze Statues.—An admirable representation of the Sleeping Faun, from Herculaneum; two Discoboli, or quoit-players, watching the result of a throw (Herculaneum); the Dancing Faun, an exquisite conception, found in the so-called House of the Faun at Pompeii; a beautiful group of Bacchus and Ampelus, from the House of Pansa—it was found, with some other objects of importance, in a dyer's caldron, and had evidently been wrapped up in a linen fabric, the owner hoping to carry it with him in his flight from the city; colossal statue of Augustus as Jupiter; a Drunken Faun, and a life-size Mercury in repose—very beautiful in idea, and not less beautiful in execution—both were discovered at Herculaneum; a small figure of Apollo (from Pompeii), holding in one hand the lyre, in the other a plectrum—

the eyes are of silver; Alexander the Great mounted on his favourite horse, Bucephalus—a vigorous composition of high artistic excellence (from Herculaneum); Claudius Onesus (from Herculaneum); and Fortune planted on a globe (from Pompeii).

Among the smaller bronzes, chiefly excavated at Pompeii, I may mention:—

A candelabrum of exquisite design, three feet in height. At the corner of a rectangular base stands a rich angular pillar, surmounted by a capital, and adorned with a comic mask on one side, and a bull's head, with the Greek

BRONZE CANDELABRA.

word Βυκρανιον (bucranior, bovis cranium), on the other. Four decorated branches project from the angles of the abacus, and from these the lamps are suspended. The plinth, or base, is inlaid with silver ornament, vine-leaves, grapes, and fruit; the leaves in silver, the stems and fruit in a glittering brass. On one side is a naked Bacchus, his plaited locks garlanded with ivy, riding on a panther, and lifting a drinking cup in his right hand. On the other, an altar, with a fire burning upon it. The whole has a singularly graceful and charming effect. It was found in the House of Diomedes.

Ladies' toilette articles.—These comprise ear-rings, some with and some without pearl pendants; square and round mirrors of polished metal; breast-pins; rings with serpents' heads; necklaces; pots for rouge; combs, hair-pins, and bodkins of ivory.

HOUSEHOLD TREASURES.

Kitchen utensils.—Here you will see portable cooking-stoves, jelly-moulds fashioned in imitation of birds and animals, scales and weights, caldrons, saucepans, frying-pans, lamps, lamp-stands, tripods, and such a variety of pots as might gratify the cupidity of the most avaricious English housewife.

There may also be found in this collection numerous specimens of latches, locks, keys, door-hinges, bolts, screws, stirrups, bridles, thimbles, distaffs, spindles, writing materials, bells, vases, military trophies, flesh-hooks, braziers—in a word, of almost every article that entered into the economy of the daily life of antiquity. And it may be asserted, as the conclusion to be drawn from their examination, that they exhibit in a remarkable manner the ancient love of elegance and grace, while demonstrating how far inferior in fitness and ingenuity the best of them are to modern contrivances.

Glass and Terra-cotta.—I have already alluded to the absurdity of the notion which long prevailed, that the ancients were ignorant of glass. The Naples Collection contains upwards of four thousand specimens, including almost every article that could be fashioned in this material, from a luminous semi-transparent vase (discovered in the House of Diomedes), of artistic design and graceful execution, to a common window-pane. In terra-cotta the articles manufactured are of even greater variety. Here is the amphora, in which "fine old crusty wine" was preserved; the money-box in which the young Lucullus or the child Aglaia stored away their savings; the dishes which held at table the Ambracian kid or the murœna from some celebrated fish-pond; the lamps which lit up the tablinum, the atrium, or the cubicula; the votive statuettes offered by the devout at the shrines of their favourite deities; and the sepulchral urns which finally contained the ashes of the dead. You may ascend from the cellar and the kitchen to the boudoir and the banqueting-room, and find an abundant store of articles suitable for each apartment. The ancient potters must surely have been men of substance, from the extraordinary demand which prevailed for their wares.

To notice the *Gold and Silver Ornaments*, worn by the dandies and beauties of Pompeii, or employed to decorate the houses of the wealthy; to describe the vases and the cameos, the tripods and the bas-reliefs, the gems and intaglios, which have been found among its ruins, would be simply impossible, even if I restricted myself to the dull baldness of a catalogue. I can only say that they throw an important light on the arts, manners, and customs of antiquity, and brighten up many allusions in the classic writers which otherwise would baffle us by their obscurity. In conclusion, therefore, I shall content myself with a reference to the Papyri, discovered in 1752 in a suburban villa at Herculaneum. These are formed of thin laminæ, or layers, of the vegetable tissue of the papyrus reed,* so cemented together with a kind of glue as to form a long narrow sheet, varying from eight to sixteen inches in breadth, and polished in such a manner as to provide a suitable surface for the reception of the ink—a black liquid applied by means of a reed or *calamus*. The number of papyri exceeds seventeen hundred and fifty, and of these nearly a third have been unrolled and deciphered. Among them are two books of a treatise "De Natura," by Epicurus, and essays or discourses on Music and Rhetoric by Philodomus. Those hitherto deciphered have been published in a work entitled "Herculanensium Voluminum quæ supersunt."†

* A plant of the genus *Cyperus*, indigenous to Egypt
† "Edinburgh Review," October 1862.

"FINIS CORONAT OPUS."

Nearly all the MSS. have lost their first leaves, but the titles are repeated at the end. They are written in columns from three to four inches wide; each column containing from twenty to forty lines, and separated from another by a space of about an inch. The sentences are not distinguished by stops of any kind.

The above imperfect list includes the more notable discoveries made in the buried cities of Campania, and is sufficient, at all events, to convey to the reader's mind a tolerably accurate idea of their intrinsic value and archæological importance.

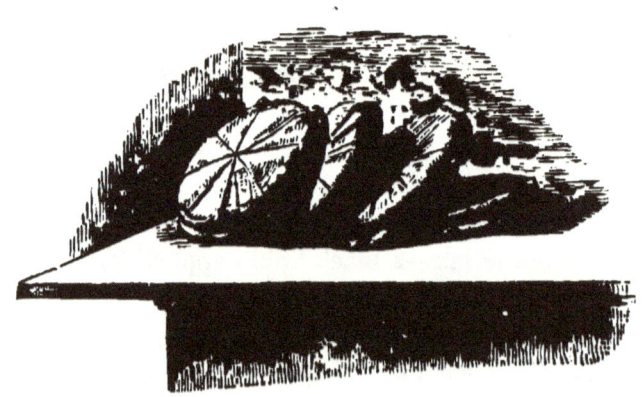

BREAD DISCOVERED AT POMPEII.

INDEX.

ACTORS of Greece and Rome, 127, 128.
Æola, Isle of, 12.
Ærarium, the, uses of, 77.
Alcobierre, his excavations at Pompeii, 48.
Amalfi, 12.
Amphitheatres, when first erected, 108; history of, 109; description of, 109, 110; their interior arrangements, 111, 112; laws and institutions of, 112, 113; at Pompeii, 122-125.
Amusements, Greek and Roman, character of, 103.
Andabatæ, the, 105.
Appian, cited, 18.
Atrium, the, in a Roman house, described, 93.
Auctorati, the, 104.
Augustales, the, described, 85.
Avernus, Lake of, 13, 24.

BASILICA, the, description of, 74-77; origin of, 74; dimensions, 77; constitution of, 75; interior, 76.
Bas-reliefs at Pompeii, 113, 121.
Baths, the Roman, description of, 152, et seq.; vast extent of, 153-156; inauguration of, 155, 156; the apodyterium, 157; decorations of the apartments, 158; the frigidarium, 159-161; the tepidarium, 161-167; the calidarium, 167-169; the Women's Baths, 170, 171; the New Baths at Pompeii, 171, 172; bathing processes described, 173-175; oils and unguents, 176; perfumes and cosmetics, 176, 177; minor arrangements, 177.
Beattie, Dr. W., quoted, 252.
Bekker, cited, 138, 162, 238.
Bellaria, the, 92.
Blacas collection, the, 258.
Brand, quoted, 223.

Burial rites amongst the Romans, 237, 238; ceremonies of interment described, 238-241.
Byron, quoted, 152.

CÆNA, a Roman, details of, 91, 92.
Cænacula, the, described, 91.
Caligula, anecdote of, 125.
Campania, its volcanic activity, 24; early legends of, 24.
Caricatures, Pompeian, specimens of, 20.
Cassius, Dion, cited, 107.
Catullus, quoted, 180.
Chalcidium, the, description and history of, 77-81.
Chapman, the poet, quoted, 97.
Commodus, anecdote of, 125.
Cumæ, 13.

DIMACHERI, the, 105.
Dobell, Sydney, quoted, 152.
Domestic articles discovered at Pompeii, 274-276.
Donaldson, cited, 61.
Dyer, Dr., quoted, 21, 42, 211, 212.

EATING-HOUSE, a Pompeian, 261-263.
Elbœuf, Prince d', reference to, 43.
Ennemoser, quoted, 150.
Equites, the, 105.
Essedari, the, 105.
Eumachia, statue of, 79.
Eustace, quoted, 154.
Excavations at Pompeii, how conducted, 258-261.

FORUM, the Pompeian, 62; its frequenters, 62-65, 72, 73; description of, 65; its temples, 66-71.
Frescoes, mythological, description of, 151, 185, 211, 270-272.
Fullonica, the, described, 206-209.

Funeral Triclinium, the, described, 244, 245.

GARUM, a pickle so called, 59.
Gates, the Pompeian, described, 49-51.
Gell, Sir William, quoted, 66, 68, 78, 84, 90, 97, 155, 159, 170, 176, 198, 199, 220.
Gibbon, quoted, 109, 110.
Gladiators, first exhibited, 104; whence obtained, 104; various classes of, 104-106; shows of, described, 106, 108, 111, 112; laws of gladiatorial combats, 112, 113; sculptures representing, 113-121.
Graffiti, the, 56.
Granaries, the, 68.
Gustatio, the, 91.

HEMICYCLES, their nature and uses, 249, 250.
Herculaneum, its ancient splendour, 14; its destruction, 15, 16, 22; its origin and early history, 22, 23; excavations in, 43; re-discovery of, 252; ruins at, 253; theatre of, 253, 254; its past and present contrasted, 255.
Homer, quoted, 13, 24, 89, 196.
Hoplomachi, the, 105.
Horace, quoted, 86, 113, 135, 155, 184.
Houses at Pompeii, description of, 180-187; general arrangements, 189, 190; the atrium and tablinum, 181; alæ, fauces, compluvium, 182; peristyle and cubicula, 183; triclinium, 183-187; oeci and exedræ, 187; pinacotheca and bibliotheca, 188; balneum, 188.
Houses, of the Sculptor, 145, 146; the Tragic Poet, 190-202; of Ceres, 203, 204; the Fountains, 204-206; Holconius, 209-212; Pansa, 212-217; Sallust, 217-219; the Dioscuri, 219-222; the Centaur, 223.

ISEON, the, description of, 146-150.
Isis, worship of, 150.

JUVENAL, quoted, 92, 112, 177.

KAVANAGH, Miss, quoted, 255.

LAQUEATORES, the, 105.
Liternum, 13.
Lucan, quoted, 110.
Lucretius, quoted, 103.
Ludi amphitheatrales, description of the, 103-126.
Lytton, Lord, quoted, 51, 52, 73, 74.

MARSTON, quoted, 223.
Martial, quoted, 14, 176.

Mazois, cited, 184, 248.
Milton, quoted, 12.
Mirmillones, the, 105.
Misenum, 12.
Monnier, M. Marc, quoted, 69, 264.
Mosaic, illustrative of domestic arrangements, 130.
Mosaics at Pompeii, 272.

NAPLES, Bay of, 11; beauty of, 11; commercial advantages of, 16; ancient prosperity of, 17; Oscan colonies of, 17.

ORNAMENTS discovered at Pompeii, 277.
Overbeck, quoted, 43, 47, 57, 58, 69, 76, 84, 87, 115, 118, 137, 139, 145, 162, 169, 173, 209, 215, 242, 243, 247, 269.

PÆSTUM, 12.
Paintings discovered at Pompeii, 194-200.
Papyri at Pompeii, 277, 278.
Persius, quoted, 174.
Pindar, cited, 17.
Pistor, shop of a, described, 59.
Pliny, his account of the eruption of Vesuvius, 27-36; cited, 59.
Pompeii, ancient magnificence of, 14; present desolation, 15; destruction of, 15, 16; its origin, 17; early history, 18; captured by Sulla, 18; a Roman colony, 18, 19; quarrel with Nuceria, 19, 20; its caricatures, 20; its wealth, 21; description of its ruin, 27-42; attempted restoration by Nero, 42; early excavations at, 42, 43; by the Neapolitan government, 44, 45; royal visits to the buried city, 45, 46; its geographical position, 47, 48; its environs, 48; its walls, 48, 49; its gates, 49-51; its streets, 51-53; its street-literature, 54-58; its shops, 58-61; the Forum, 62-96; its amphitheatre and public games, 103-126; its theatres, 127-143; its barracks, 143-145; its public buildings, 145-151; its Thermæ, or Baths, 152-178; its houses, 179-223; its streets, 223-234; its tombs, 237-251; recent discoveries at, 256-268.

RETIARII, the, 106.
Rimmel, quoted, 176.
Rogers, quoted, 11, 12, 62.

SCULPTURES at Pompeii, 273.
Secutores, the, 106.
Senaculum, the, described, 83, 84.
Shakspeare, quoted, 127.
Shelley, quoted, 47.

LIST OF ILLUSTRATIONS. 281

Skeletons at Pompeii, discovery of, 265-268.
Soldiers' Barracks, the, described, 143, 144.
Sorrento, 12.
Spartianus, quoted, 175.
Stabiæ, position of, 23; early history of, 23; under the Romans, 23.
Statues in bronze at Pompeii, 273, 274.
Strabo, references to, 17, 24.
Streets of Pompeii, described and particularized, 51-53, 223, *et seq.*; Street of Domitian, 52; of Abundance, 52; of Fortune, 52: of Nola, 52; of Fortune, 101: of Herculaneum, 223, 224; of Narcissus, 225; of Modestus, 225; of the Fullonica, 225; of the Mercuries, 225-229; of the Faun, 229; of the Baths, 230, 231; of Stabiæ, 231-233.
Suetonius, cited, 19.
Sulla, capture of Pompeii by, 18.

Tasso, Torquato, reference to, 12.
Temples of Pompeii, account of, 66, *et in multis locis*; of Jupiter, 66, 67; of Venus, 69-71; of Quirinus, 81-83; of Fortune, 97-102; of Hercules, 134-136; of Æsculapius, 145; of Isis, 146-150.
Tennyson, quoted, 21.
Theatre, a Roman, described, 128, 129; scena and proscenium, 129, 130; pulpitum and orchestra, 131; scenery

of, 131, 132; dramas represented in, 132, 133; historical sketch of, 133, 134.
Theatres of Pompeii, described, 134, 135; the Great Theatre, 137; interior of do., 138-140; the Little Theatre, or Odeum, 141; internal arrangements of, 141-143.
Thermopolium, a, described, 60.
Tholos, a, described, 93.
Tibullus, quoted, 237.
Tombs of Pompeii, account of, 237; of Diomedes, 241, 242; of Cenis and Labeo, 242; of the Libellæ, 243; Tomb with the Marble Door, 243; of Næ-voleia Tyche, 245, 246; of the Istacidian family, 246; of Calventius Quietus, 247, 248; of Patricius Scaurus, 248; of Tyche, 248; of the Glass Amphora, 248; of the Garlands, 249; of Terentius Felix, 249; of the Priestess Mamia, 250.
Tribunal, the, 150.
Typhon, legend of, 24.

Venationes, the, history and account of, 106-108.
Vesuvius, the mountain, grandeur of, 13; various eruptions of, 15, 24, 27; legends connected with, 24; annals of, 27; great eruption of, described by Pliny, 27-36.
Virgil, quoted, 12, 32, 129, 182, 241.
Vitruvius, quoted, 189.

LIST OF ILLUSTRATIONS.

[*The Italics indicate whole-page Engravings.*]

Page
1. *Frontispiece—View of Vesuvius from the Site of Pompeii.*
2. A Pompeian Caricature 20
3. *Mount Vesuvius previous to the Eruption of A.D. 63* 25
4. *Mount Vesuvius after the Eruption* 38
5. Street of Sallust (Strada di Sallustio) 53
6. Graffite, or Wall Caricature 56
7. A Baker's Shop 59
8. Thermopolium......................60
9. Section of do......................61
10. *Forum of Pompeii*..............63
11. *Temple of Venus*................69
12. Fresco found at Pompeii.........72
13. Statues of Livia and Drusus 88
14. *Temple of Fortune restored*......98

Page
15. Specimen of Marbles found at Pompeii....................101
16. Combat between a Veles and a Samnite....................117
17. Combat between a Thracian and a Mirmillo 118
18. Combat between a Mirmillo and a Samnite.................120
19. Combat between a Light-armed Gladiator and a Samnite.....120
20. Arming for the Combat.........122
21. Curricle or Chariot Bar for two Horses....................125
22. Mosaic: Actors instructed by the Choragus................130
23. Masks, Dwarf, and Monkey....133
24. Comic Scene...................140
25. *Fresco: A Landscape*..........142

LIST OF ILLUSTRATIONS.

	Page
26. Mythological Frescoes	151
27. The Frigidarium	160
28. View of the Tepidarium	163
29. Ceiling of the Tepidarium	166
30. Ornaments of the Tepidarium	167
31. Calidarium	168
32. A Wine-cart	178
33. Female Centaur and Bacchante	185
34. Male Centaur and Bacchante	185
35. An Ancient Galley	188
36. *House of the Tragic Poet*	191
37. Cave Canem!	193
38. Achilles delivers Briseis to the Heralds of Ajax	195
39. Head of Achilles	196
40. Sacrifice of Iphigenia	201
41. Fullers at Work	207
42. Ancient Fullers	208
43. Bacchus and Ariadne	211
44. *Atrium of the House of Pausa*	213
45. Jupiter and his Eagle	220
46. Court in the House of the Quæstor	222
47. Achilles at the Court of Lycomedes	226
48. Allegorical Figure	227
49. *View of the Villa of Diomedes*	235
50. *Street of Tombs*	239
51. Street at Pompeii recently explored	250
52. Bodies discovered among the Ruins of Pompeii	266
53. Body discovered among the Ruins of Pompeii	267
54. Achilles instructed by Chiron to Play upon the Lyre	271
55. Bronze Candelabra	274
56. Household Treasures	275
57. Bread discovered at Pompeii	278
Plan of Pompeii	13

Nelson's Art Gift-Books.

AN ENTIRELY NEW SERIES OF FIRST-CLASS AND RICHLY ILLUSTRATED

WORKS ON PHYSICAL SCIENCE.

---o---

THE BIRD. By JULES MICHELET, Author of "History of France," &c. Illustrated by Two Hundred and Ten Exquisite Engravings by GIACOMELLI. Imperial 8vo, full gilt side and gilt edges. Price 10s. 6d.

WESTMINSTER REVIEW.—"*This work consists of an exposition of various ornithological matters from points of view which could hardly be thought of, except by a writer of Michelet's peculiar genius. With his argument in favour of the preservation of our small birds we heartily concur. The translation seems to be generally well executed; and in the matter of paper and printing, the book is almost an ouvrage de luxe. The illustrations are generally very beautiful.*"

THE MYSTERIES OF THE OCEAN. From the French of ARTHUR MANGIN. By the Translator of "The Bird." With One Hundred and Thirty Illustrations by W. FREEMAN and J. NOEL. Imperial 8vo, full gilt side and gilt edges. Price 10s. 6d.

PALL MALL GAZETTE.—"*Science walks to-day in her silver slippers. We have here another sumptuously produced popular manual from France. It is an account, complete in extent and tolerably full in detail, of the Sea. It is eminently readable....The illustrations are altogether excellent; and the production of such a book proves at least that there are very many persons who can be calculated on for desiring to know something of physical science.*"

THE DESERT WORLD. From the French of ARTHUR MANGIN. Translated, Edited, and Enlarged by the Translator of "The Bird" by Michelet. With One Hundred and Sixty Illustrations by W. FREEMAN, FOULQUIER, and YAN D'ARGENT. Imperial 8vo, full gilt. Price 12s. 6d.

BRITISH QUARTERLY REVIEW.—"*The wonders of natural phenomena are unfolded with a graceful and poetic pen, and are skilfully illustrated by the artist's pencil, so that the sentiment of wonder is fed by both imagination and art. It is a charming and very attractive book.*"

EARTH AND SEA. From the French of LOUIS FIGUIER. Translated, Edited, and Enlarged by W. H. DAVENPORT ADAMS. Illustrated with Two Hundred and Fifty Engravings by FREEMAN, GIACOMELLI, YAN D'ARGENT, PRIOR, FOULQUIER, RIOU, LAPLANTE, and other Artists. Imperial 8vo. Handsomely bound in cloth and gold. Price 12s. 6d.

SATURDAY REVIEW.—"*This is another of those handsome and popular science manuals, profusely and beautifully illustrated, of which so many have been recently published in France. The English editor and translator has frequently expanded and improved his original, which exhibits much research. Physical geography has not often been so picturesquely treated, and the English publishers are to be congratulated on this volume.*"

T. NELSON AND SONS, LONDON, EDINBURGH, AND NEW YORK.

Art Gift-Books for the Young.

THE WORLD AT HOME: Pictures and Scenes from Far-off Lands. By MARY and ELIZABETH KIRBY. With upwards of One Hundred and Thirty Illustrations. Small 4to, cloth, richly gilt. Price 6s.

THE TIMES.—"*An admirable collection of adventures and incidents in foreign lands, gleaned largely from foreign sources, and excellently illustrated.*"

BRITISH QUARTERLY REVIEW.—"*A very charming book; one of the best popular wonder-books for young people that we have seen. In language of singular simplicity, and with a very profuse use of very effective woodcuts, the distinctive features of far-off lands—their natural history, the manners and customs of their inhabitants, their physical phenomena, &c.—are brought home to the fireside in a way to entrance alike the children of five or six years old, and the older folk who instruct them. No better book has appeared this season.*"

COMPANION VOLUME TO "THE WORLD AT HOME."

THE SEA AND ITS WONDERS. By MARY and ELIZABETH KIRBY. With One Hundred and Seventy-four Illustrations. Small 4to, cloth, richly gilt. Price 6s.

MORNING POST.—"*If literary and artistic effect can induce one to take to the study of Nature's Book, this work ought to prevail.*"

Beautifully Illustrated by Giacomelli, Illustrator of "The Bird" by Michelet.

BIRDS AND FLOWERS. By MARY HOWITT. With Eighty-four Original Illustrations. Crown 8vo. Handsomely bound in cloth and gold. Price 6s.

SATURDAY REVIEW.—"*The illustrations are true to nature, and full of spirit.*"

ILLUSTRATED LONDON NEWS.—"*An extremely pretty book. Mrs. Howitt's graceful little poems are worthily accompanied by such refined specimens of graphic art, at once truthful and delightful.*"

NELSON'S HOUSEHOLD SERIES OF STANDARD FAVOURITES.

THE HOUSEHOLD ROBINSON CRUSOE, CAREFULLY REPRINTED FROM THE ORIGINAL EDITION.

THE LIFE AND STRANGE ADVENTURES OF ROBINSON CRUSOE, OF YORK, MARINER. WRITTEN BY HIMSELF. WITH AN INTRODUCTORY MEMOIR OF DANIEL DE FOE, A MEMOIR OF ALEXANDER SELKIRK, AN ACCOUNT OF PETER SERRANO, and other Interesting Additions.

Illustrated with upwards of Seventy Engravings by KEELEY HALSWELLE, a Portrait of De Foe, a Map of Crusoe's Island, De Foe's Tomb, Facsimiles of Original Title-Pages, &c. &c. Crown 8vo, cloth extra, gilt edges. Price 6s.

THE HOUSEHOLD SWISS FAMILY ROBINSON, A NEW AND UNABRIDGED TRANSLATION OF THE ORIGINAL.

THE SWISS FAMILY ROBINSON; or, Adventures of a Shipwrecked Family on a Desolate Island. A New and Unabridged Translation. With an Introduction from the French of CHARLES NODIER. Illustrated with upwards of Three Hundred Engravings. Crown 8vo, cloth extra. Price 6s.

THE SPECTATOR.—"*We never met the child yet whom this story did not fascinate; and if some publisher would have it translated in its old fulness, we believe it would have a success like that of 'Uncle Tom's Cabin.'*"

T. NELSON AND SONS, LONDON, EDINBURGH, AND NEW YORK.

www.ingramcontent.com/pod-product-compliance
Lightning Source LLC
Chambersburg PA
CBHW032107230426
43672CB00009B/1658